WHO
INVENTED THE
BICYCLE
KICK?

SOCCER'S GREATEST
LEGENDS AND LORE

PAUL SIMPSON &
ULI HESSE

WILLIAM MORROW

An Imprint of HarperCollins*Publishers*

HarperCollins books may be purchased for educational, business, or sales promotional use. For information, please e-mail the Special Markets Departments at SPsales@harpercollins.com.

First published as *Who Invented the Stepover?* in Great Britain in 2013 by Profile Books LTD.

FIRST U.S. EDITION

Library of Congress Cataloging-in-Publication Data has been applied for.

ISBN 978-0-06-234694-0

14 15 16 17 18 OV/RRD 10 9 8 7 6 5 4 3 2 1

For Yannick and Jack, who'll never walk alone

Contents

Stars

Gaffers

Records

Culture

Introduction

Who invented the stepover? The thought must have occurred to many of us while watching Cristiano Ronaldo taunt an opponent with this trick. Maradona, perhaps? Pelé? Surely some South American. I was editing *Champions* magazine, so did some initial research and traced the trick back to a Dutch footballer called Abe Lenstra in the 1950s. But there the trail went cold. Picking up the investigation for this book, the answer became much more complex and entertaining, touching on the careers of Bob Marley, a player celebrated as 'Adam the Scissors Man' and a Boca Juniors legend who played in espadrilles instead of football boots.

That question, inevitably, led to other conundrums – who invented the bicycle kick and the long throw, who had the hardest ever shot, what was the greatest of all great escapes, what is the point of corner flags and dugouts, and just where did all those football pop singles come from? I'd always found the *New Scientist* question and answer books, such as *Why Can't Elephants Jump?*, curiously addictive and began to wonder if a similar approach would shed new light on the game of football – its origins, development and culture. When my co-author Uli Hesse suggested that one of the questions we could answer was 'Can elephants take penalties?', it seemed excitingly obvious that it could.

The selection of questions posed and, in general, answered here has led us into various corridors of uncertainty, sharpened our reading of the game and left us still pondering the connection between parrots, football and misery. They have also introduced us to a fascinating gallery of characters – the German coach who was shot in the jaw while sharing a bed with a suspected CIA agent, the striker who used to smoke dollar bills at half-time, and a doomed Dutch prodigy who learned how to beat defenders by watching people speed skate over frozen canals – who barely feature in the orthodox version of football's rise to become the most popular sport in the world.

Along the way we also consider the synergy between tobacco and football, the mysterious origins of 4-4-2 and whether Argentina would have won the 1986 World Cup without Maradona. (Not the toughest question we had to answer.) The end result is a book that shreds shibboleths, challenges assumptions and could inspire a truly epic pub quiz – or possibly incite a riot at one.

Paul Simpson, October 2013

Inventions

🄯 Who invented the bicycle kick?

If you believe Uruguayan writer Eduardo Galeano's *Football In Sun and Shadow*, this question has a straightforward answer. To quote Galeano: 'Ramón Unzaga invented the move on the field of the Chilean port Talcahuano: body in the air, back to the ground, he shot the ball backwards with a sudden snap of his legs, like the blades of scissors.'

Galeano does not date this historic moment but popular tradition has it that Unzaga invented this move in 1914 in Talcahuano. A naturalised Chilean – he had emigrated from Bilbao with his parents in 1906 – Unzaga loved launching bicycle kicks both in attack and defence. After he showed off his trademark move in two Copa Americas (1916 and 1920), the Argentinian press dubbed the bicycle kick *la chilena*.

As comprehensive as that narrative might sound it finds no favour in Callao (Peru's largest port), nor with Argentine journalist Jorge Barraza, whose investigations suggest the move was invented by a *chalaco* (as Callao locals are known) of African descent who tried out the acrobatic manoeuvre in a game with British sailors. Peruvian historian Jorge Bazadre suggests this could have happened as early as 1892. The Chileans could, Barraza speculated, have copied the bicycle kick from regular matches between teams from Callao and the Chilean port of Valparaíso. If you believe this theory, the bicycle kick is truly *la chalaca* (Chalacan strike).

In his 1963 novel *The Time Of The Hero*, Mario Vargas Llosa suggests that people in Callao must have invented the bicycle kick because they use their feet as efficiently as their hands. However, neither Chile nor Peru will ever relinquish their claim to have invented this spectacular move. Which, when you think about it, is strange, because a bicycle kick presupposes that somebody else has not done their job properly. German scientist Hermann Schwameder, an expert on motion technique, says what you need is 'instinct, a lot of

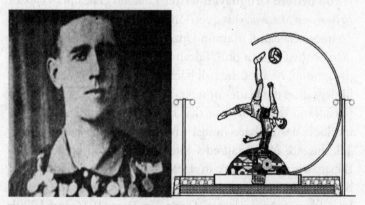

The much-decorated Chilean Ramón Unzaga, putative inventor of the bicycle kick. The equipment, right, is not recommended for home use.

courage – and a bad cross'. Klaus Fischer, who scored with the most famous bicycle kick in World Cup history (it tied the 1982 semi-final between France and West Germany at 3-3 in extra time) agrees: 'By and large, you have to say that every cross that leads to a bicycle kick goal is not a good cross.'

Yet, on one famous occasion, a not very good penalty led to a bicycle kick goal. In May 2010, in the Hungarian top flight, Honved were 1-0 up against their great rivals Ferencvaros, when they won a penalty. Italian striker Angelo Vaccaro stepped up to seal the victory. He struck the ball at a perfect height for the keeper who punched it into the air. Vaccaro waited for the ball to come down and, with half an eye on the on-rushing defenders, flicked it over his head (and the keeper) and into the net.

Even if you don't miss a penalty first, a good bicycle kick is a shortcut to glory – though sometimes that glory is short-lived. Zlatan Ibrahimović's overhead wonder goal against England in November 2012 was feted as one of the greatest ever. That same month, trying to replicate his effort in a French Cup tie for PSG against Saint-Étienne, he missed the ball completely.

Wayne Rooney's spectacular overhead kick in the Manchester derby in February 2011 was voted the best goal in the history of the Premier League. The player didn't romanticise his achievement, saying: 'I saw it come into the box and thought, why not?' Therein, perhaps, lies the secret of the move's enduring appeal: it is rare in life that we see human error (a bad cross) so swiftly redeemed by human genius.

Even a missed bicycle kick can have unforeseen consequences. At USA 94, with the hosts minutes away from a 2-1 victory against Colombia, Marcelo Balboa startled the Rose Bowl crowd with an inspired bicycle kick that flashed just over the left-hand corner. If it had gone in, it would have become one of football's most famous YouTube clips. It didn't

Rooney pulls it off. His great bicycle kick against City was improvised from a mis-hit cross from Nani. The move is said to have been introduced to England in the 1960s by United's Denis Law, who had picked it up at Torino.

but it still inspired Denver billionaire Philip Anschutz who vowed: 'That's the guy I want to play for my team.' Balboa was signed by Anschutz's Colorado Rapids and the billionaire became such an enthusiast he invested in the Chicago Fire, New York/New Jersey Metro Stars, the LA Galaxy, DC United and the San José Earthquakes – six out of ten Major League Soccer franchises. So you could say Balboa's bicycle kick launched the MLS.

There are other, less convincing, claimants for the honour of inventing the bicycle kick. Legendary Brazilian striker Leônidas, whose elasticity earned him the nickname Rubber Man, claimed the move was his creation. But he first used it, records suggest, for his club Bonsucesso in 1932 – more than a decade after Unzaga. Chronology counts even more decisively against Carlo Parola, the Juventus centre-back who used the trick so often he was known in Italy as Signor Rovesciata (Mr Reverse Kick) and Doug Ellis, the 'deadly' Aston Villa chairman who claimed to have invented this move while playing for Southport during World War II.

By then, though, the bicycle kick had achieved international notoriety. In 1927, Chilean club Colo Colo toured Europe and their 24-year-old striker, captain and founder David Arellano performed the trick so often he was the toast of Spain – until he was killed, struck down by peritonitis after colliding with another player during a match in Valladolid. The black line above Colo Colo's club emblem is a memorial to a flamboyant striker whose memorably premature death is a grim warning about the perils of showboating.

⚽ Who recorded the first celebratory football song?

Regal Records in 1932: the first FA Cup final souvenir disc was a 78rpm record commemorating the clash between Arsenal and Newcastle. This first entry in a genre we might call FA Cup vinyl was very different to its successors. For a start, the record was released before the final. And instead of the catchy, platitudinous pop songs that became obligatory, this record consisted of interviews with the players. Each finalist had a side of the record to themselves.

Controversial it isn't. The announcer, who sounds as if he's killing time before narrating his next Pathé newsreel, introduces the Gunners 'popular captain Tom Parker ... the right full-back, a wholehearted player, who is respected by his colleagues and opponents throughout the football world,

and is equally as a good a fellow.' Parker then describes the recording as a greater ordeal than anything that Wembley has to offer before promising that his team will play the game and play it well. (In the event, they lost 2-1, with Newcastle equalising controversially from a move during which the ball had gone out of play.)

There was then a strange lull before the vinyl baton was picked up in France, Germany and the Netherlands. Before the Bundesliga was founded in 1963, the national championship was decided by a cup final. In 1959, a composer called Horst Heinz Henning decided to celebrate the fact that local rivals Eintracht Frankfurt and Kickers Offenbach had reached the final by releasing a record which had an Eintracht song on one side and a Kickers tune on the other. A one-man hit factory with more pen names than Jonathan King, Henning never showed a trace of humour in his songs but, in 1977, surprised everyone by releasing a record called 'The House At The Arse End Of Nowhere'.

Neither team were involved in this commemoration of a 'dream final', but a point had been proved. In 1965, Borussia Dortmund won the Cup Winners' Cup, the first time a German club had won a European competition, and the team were inspired to record two songs. One was the Dortmund club song 'Wir Halten Fest Und Treu Zusammen' (which translates as 'We stick together firmly and faithfully') while the other was a popular carnival song from the early 1950s.

Two years later, French singer Antoine was so inspired by Ajaccio's surprising promotion to Ligue 1 he wrote and

released 'Le Match De Football'. After a downbeat opening in which the football-supporting farmer wishes his cows
would give him wine instead of milk, the song mysteriously
notes that life is sweet, going badly, yet will be redeemed by
the football on Sunday which he will watch on TV, dreaming
of the fantastic day when the Corsicans win the Olympics.
The song was the main attraction on an EP with a lovely old-
school cover featuring a classic team photo.

In 1970, as the tuxedoed members of the England World
Cup squad were singing 'They'll be thinking about us back
home', Feyenoord celebrated winning the European Cup
with their own single. The golden – if that's the appropriate
metal to be invoking – age of the celebratory record had just
started. Arsenal, Brighton, Bristol City, Cardiff City, Chelsea,
Coventry City, Crystal Palace, Everton, Leeds United, Lincoln City, Manchester United, Middlesbrough, Nottingham
Forest, Scotland, Spurs and Yeovil have all graced – or disgraced – the charts with their ditties. So popular were these
singles that Chelsea recorded 'Blue Is The Colour' in 1972
just to celebrate the fact that they had reached the League Cup
final (which they lost to Stoke City). 'Blue Is The Colour' has
since been adapted (although the colour has often changed)
by the Vancouver Whitecaps,
Norwegian champions Molde
and Finnish giants HJK.

Apart from the classic
'Anfield Rap' and the almost-
credible 'World In Motion'
(New Order with John Barnes),
most of these cash-in singles
were cheesily predictable. It
took the Belgians to show Britain how these things should be

ANTOINE

LE MATCH DE FOOTBALL
LES TOITS DE MON VILLAGE VENEZ AVEC NOUS HIVER

done. In 1985 Belgian singer Grand Jojo, best known for his drinking songs, cut 'Anderlecht Champions' with the Mauves squad that had just won the Belgian title. The first verse features the usual platitudes about growing up as a fan but in the second verse, the song takes a bizarre, entertaining diversion in which the singer complains that he went to see another team, but there wasn't even a cat nearby and the car park was deserted. The baffled fan sings: 'But in front of me there were three turnstiles open. At one of the turnstiles I said: "Has the match been put off until Easter or Christmas?" The bloke in front of me said, "Don't worry mate! As you've come on your own, we'll start whenever you want!"'

It's an old gag but it is surely better than, for example, 'And we'll play all the way for Leeds United'.

⚽ Who invented 4-4-2?

The orthodox view is that the classic 4-4-2 formation was invented by Victor Maslov. Jonathan Wilson's *Inverting The Pyramid* makes this case eloquently, noting: '[Sir Alf] Ramsey is regularly given the credit (or the blame) for abolishing the winger and, given the lack of communication between the USSR and the West in those days, there is no suggestion he did not come up with the idea independently, but the 4-4-2 was first invented by Maslov.'

This invention was perfected at Dynamo Kiev, coached by Maslov from 1964 to 1970. Looking at the 4-3-3 with which Brazil had won the 1962 World Cup with forward Mário Zagallo falling back on the left, Maslov decided to go one better and pulled back his right-winger too. The idea was to give his players, especially his playmaker Andriy Biba, the freedom to create. But just as Ramsey dispensed with tricky wingers (because they held on to the ball too long), so Maslov parted with his gifted winger Valeriy Lobanovskiy. The 4-4-2 Maslov created was, in part, a formal shape that made it possible for his players to interchange because they knew which shape they had to keep. A defender pressing forward in this system knew a team-mate would cover the space he had left. Without that structure, the team could not be creative and remain competitive.

Coaches whose experiments succeed are regarded as deep thinkers, those whose ploys don't pay off are derided as 'tink-erers'. Yet as Maslov's reign in Kiev shows, great coaches are usually both. By October 1967, when his team knocked out European champions Celtic in the first round of the European Cup, Maslov had his side playing 4-1-3-2 with Vasili Turian-chik as a holding midfielder sitting in front of the back four.

Oddly enough, as Wilson points out in his book, this is probably the most accurate description of the formation with which Ramsey's England won the 1966 World Cup final. In front of the back four was Nobby Stiles, playing behind a midfield trio of Alan Ball, Bobby Charlton and Martin Peters, with Geoff Hurst and Roger Hunt as the attacking two.

Yet tactically the most significant matches in that tournament might well have been in Group 1. The scoreline in England's routine 2-0 win over Mexico was a tactical triumph for coach Ignacio Trelles. In May 1961, Mexico had lost 8-0 on their first visit to Wembley. Desperate to avoid such humiliation, the players agreed to emulate Uruguay (who had held the hosts to 0-0 in the opening game) and play for a draw. 'We played them using a 4-4-2 which we weren't used to and was considered super defensive,' said Trelles. 'We gave the English a lot of work to do. Only a great goal by Bobby Charlton opened us up.' Defender Jesús del Muro, who shrugged off injury to play that game, recalled later: 'That was the day they said Nacho Trelles put out the "formation of fear", because he played 4-4-2. Imagine – in 1986, they were all playing it.'

Uruguay, under coach Ondino Viera (the man who famously observed 'other countries have their history, Uruguay has football'), also set out to play 4-4-2 against France, although this changed when they went a goal down after 15 minutes. So what we have is the spectacle, in one round of games halfway through Group 1, of two sides, Mexico and Uruguay, playing 4-4-2 for some or all of their World Cup match in 1966 – just two years after Maslov had begun experimenting with this formation in Kiev.

It is extremely unlikely – given the lack of communication between East and West that Wilson acknowledged – that either Viera or Trelles had consulted with Maslov, let alone Ramsey. The timeline may still favour the Russian coach, yet Trelles was a great tactical innovator (and was often criticised for it by the Mexican media) so it is hard to settle this argument definitively. In his book *Where Good Ideas Come From*, author Steven Johnson points out that four different scientists in four different countries all 'discovered' sunspots in the same year, 1611. His theory of innovation is that they are created not by lone geniuses but by a process he calls the 'adjacent possible'. This is his way of saying that only certain kinds of next steps are possible – you can't invent the printing press without moveable type, ink and paper.

So applying this theory, 4-4-2 became an adjacent possibility as soon as a team proved you could succeed playing 4-3-3. At its simplest, the distinction between the two is merely the positioning of one winger. Which means that almost any reasonably intelligent, open-minded coach could have studied what Brazil did in 1962 and drawn the same conclusions as Maslov, Ramsey and Trelles.

⚽ Who was the first attacking full-back?

On 15 May 1949, Arsenal beat the Brazilian side Fluminense 5-1 in the Vasco da Gama stadium in front of 60,000 excited fans. As comfortable as that margin of victory sounds, the Arsenal defenders endured much discomfort. As full-back Laurie Scott recalled in Aidan Hamilton's *An Entirely Different Game*: 'Suddenly, a bloke comes dashing through and he's had a shot at goal and the ball went wide. And we started looking around to see who we'd got to blame for this. We found out it was their full-back. See, they didn't care. I never went up there like that. I used to go down the sideline, yes, but never like that.'

As the great Dutch coach Rinus Michels famously said, the problem is not persuading full-backs to go forward, they all want to do that, the problem is to persuade them to track back. This is especially true in Brazil. So the honest answer to this question is that it could have been any Brazilian full-back at any time from the 1930s onwards.

Then again it could have been an Englishman. In the 1930s, left-back Samuel Barkas won five England caps while on Manchester City's books. In Douglas Lamming's stuffy but compelling *An English Football Internationalists' Who's Who*, he quotes a contemporary appraisal of Barkas which sums him up as 'clever and stylish with a liking for an occasional foray upfield'. It's worth noting that Barkas could have indulged this liking as a left-half and inside-right – he was good enough to play in most positions – but there is at least a possibility that he was given licence to enjoy this role.

The first gifted pioneers to make an impact on a World Cup as attacking (or overlapping, as they were called back in the 1950s) full-backs were the Hungarian right-back Jeno Buzanszky and left-back Mihály Lantos. The Hungarian duo were such paragons of virtue that even Michels would have approved. Steady, reliable and strong in the tackle, they were primed to launch counter-attacks. Buzanszky loved to dribble up the wing and cross into the centre, while Lantos had a powerful driving shot.

Hungary should have won the 1954 World Cup with their attacking full-backs. Four years later, Brazil did just that with the unrelated Djalma and Nilton Santos on the right and left of their back four. The latter had made his mark as a prolific striker, been bought by Botafogo as a reserve centre-half and then made his debut at left-back. He never really regarded his new role as purely defensive and, sweeping up the flanks like a frustrated striker, he perfected the attacking full-back role. He overlapped brilliantly with Djalma who was slightly less enterprising but still provided the cross for Brazil's third goal in the 1962 World Cup final.

By proving that goals could be made or scored from almost any position, the Santoses liberated the game tactically. Paradoxically, the most compelling proof of their enduring

Brazil's World Cup winners, 1954. Standing, from left: Djalma Santos, Zito, Gilmar, Zozimo, Nilton Santos, Mauro. Squatting: America, Garrincha, Didi, Vava, Amarildo and Zagalo.

influence was offered by Helenio Herrera's Inter Milan, who dominated European football with their counter-attacking *catenaccio* in the 1960s. When Herrera was criticised for his team's sterile tactics, he would point to the *Nerazzurri's* elegant attacking left-back, Giacinto Facchetti.

Facchetti was a full-back who wanted to be a centre-forward but put his frustration to good use, becoming, in 1971–72, the highest-scoring full-back in the history of Italian football. 'It was a trait I brought with me from my days playing at the church youth centre,' Facchetti said once. 'I didn't like to sit back, I preferred to follow the action and finish it.' Among his legion of admirers was a young centre-back called Franz Beckenbauer. 'He inspired me to play in my own style,' said the Kaiser. 'He was one of the few who turned a defensive role into an attacking one. As a left-back, he went up and down the entire wing, which made him unpredictable. He even scored goals. His options were limited – in his position he could move only straight ahead or to his right – whereas for me, in the centre, everything was possible.'

Today, football seems to be teeming with full-backs who look better going forward than running back. Some fans still pine for the old-school full-back who tackled like a beast and believed the only appropriate use of the ball was to belt it into Row Z. For the diehards, the man who must shoulder the blame is Djalma Santos. Not only was he supremely effective in attack, he was one of the first, great full-backs to prove that scything tackles were overrated, showing that you were usually better off shepherding the attacker into such a useless part of their pitch that, in their demoralised state, they could be dispossessed with ease.

Which goalie first wore gloves?

One of the great old-time goalies, Heiner Stuhlfauth, who played for Nuremberg and Germany in the 1920s, recalled: 'When it was raining, I would wear gloves made of rough wool. A wet ball will stick to such gloves. It was something I learned from life – I knew you cannot hold an eel with your bare hands, that you have to grip him using a rough piece of cloth.'

His contemporary, the Spanish keeper Ricardo Zamora, rarely stepped onto the pitch without gloves, though they may have primarily been a fashion statement. The man they called El Divino was very fastidious about his appearance. His trademark accessories were his legendary white V-neck sweater and a black turtleneck. Zamora smoked 65 cigarettes a day in the latter stages of his career and liked to calm his nerves at half-time with a quick ciggie. He never went anywhere without his good luck charm – a crude doll in a dark frock. So perhaps the well-dressed superstar simply considered gloves part of a gentleman's proper attire. However, Zamora's gloves weren't of much use on his blackest day, when Spain lost 7-1 to England in December 1931. So many balls slipped out of the divine one's grasp on a muddy Highbury pitch that one newspaper complained that Spain might as well have put Zamora's lucky charm between the sticks.

Stuhlfauth and Zamora pre-date two famous keepers who are often credited with pioneering the use of gloves in the 1940s: Charlton's Sam Bartram, and Argentinian keeper Amadeo Carrizo, both of whom are pictured with and without gloves. One famous contemporary of Carrizo's always wore gloves, the great Lev Yashin. Dubbed the Black Panther because of the colour of his kit, he looked fashionably monochrome with black gloves. Yashin wore tight leather gloves, not ones made of wool, so he wasn't wearing them to warm his hands. Indeed, after the 1956 Olympic final, Yashin approached the Yugoslav keeper, Petar Radenković, urged him to switch to wearing gloves and gave him a pair to use.

Yet none of these gloves were the special custom-made products that spread like wildfire in the 1970s. Germany's Sepp Maier is widely considered the first to wear oversized gloves with padding and rubber inlays. The move towards modern gloves began when Maier took up wearing gloves made of terry cloth instead of wool or leather. 'One day I was drying the ball with a towel and noticed it stuck to the ball,' he recalls. 'So then I had gloves made from this material.' Ultimately, Maier's experiment led to the huge gloves that

Cap, check. Gloves, check. Lev Yashin lines up, fully prepared, for the USSR, 1958.

became his trademark. Bob Wilson once said: 'I remember making fun of the big gloves Maier wore at the 1974 World Cup. Within a year, everyone was wearing them.'

John Burridge, easily as eccentric as the renowned practical joker Maier, says: 'I was the first keeper in England to wear gloves. I'd seen Sepp Maier wearing them. I had to get them from Germany; you couldn't get them in England. Pat Jennings and Peter Shilton rang me for pairs.'

Maier collaborated with Gebhard Reusch, whose father had founded a company that was producing winter sports equipment, including skiing gloves. In 1973, Reusch introduced a range of goalkeeping gloves bearing Maier's name. At roughly the same time, Wolfgang Fahrian, West Germany's goalkeeper at the 1962 World Cup, had been experimenting with cutting up the rubber sheets used on table-tennis racquets and glueing them onto gloves for a better grip. Fahrian teamed up with sportswear entrepreneur Kurt Kränzle and put out his own range. Fahrian had the same nickname as Yashin – the Black Panther – and fought Radenković for a place in 1860 Munich's goal.

Who invented the league?

No one's going to like the answer to this, so let's delay the inevitable for a while and start with some linguistics. The term 'league' comes from the Latin word 'ligare', meaning to bind, and refers to a group of people, nations or institutions bound together for and by a purpose. What we now call league football began, in 1888, when William McGregor of Aston Villa invited several professional clubs to a meeting to create an association that would organise regular, scheduled games. This organisation could have been called the Football Association, but since that name was already taken, McGregor and his associates settled on the Football League. In its inaugural year, the league was contested by twelve clubs from the north and Midlands: Accrington, Aston Villa, Blackburn Rovers, Bolton Wanderers, Burnley, Derby County, Everton, Notts County, Preston North End, Stoke F.C., West Bromwich Albion and Wolverhampton Wanderers. The winners were Preston, who were unbeaten, and also won the FA Cup.

The first-ever football league winners – Preston North End, 1889.

This derivation explains why there are football leagues that don't really play league football. Consider, for instance, the ACDV League. ACDV stands for Attività Calcistica dei Dipendenti Vaticani and refers to the Vatican City State FA. There are normally 16 teams in this league (one is called, and we're not making this up, North American Martyrs). The precise championship format varies, but usually the teams are divided into groups, from which the best teams qualify for a knock out cup tournament, the Clericus Cup, fittingly played after Easter.

But forming a league is only the first step. The next one for McGregor and his allies was designing some kind of system for a competition. We all know how it eventually turned out – each team played the other once at home and once away;

two points were awarded for a win and one for a draw – but these are just details, as the number of games, where they are played or how many points are distributed is ultimately of no relevance to what we consider a league system.

The best and shortest description of what we are looking for is this: 'A league uses a prearranged schedule of games to decide on a championship from among its members.' This definition comes from *The Dickson Baseball Dictionary*, a book that should know what it's talking about, because the league system was invented in the United States and first introduced in baseball. In America, the National League was already into its twelfth season when McGregor and the others formally created the Football League at the Royal Hotel in Manchester.

The National League, the oldest existing professional team sports league in the world, was founded on 2 February 1876, but the first professional sports league, the National Association of Professional Base Ball Players, was formed five years earlier. This association originally comprised ten clubs, nine of which fielded a team for the inaugural season. The clubs played between 27 and 35 games against each other (scheduling was still a problem). Philadelphia Athletics won the most games (22) and were declared champions. This was a league, as we understand this today, in all but name, and it was born in the same year as Marcel Proust and Orville Wright.

Of course, a league is not always a straightforward thing. In Argentina, a truly arcane system determines the clubs to be relegated, based on their average points per match over a three-year period. (Relegation, introduced by way of play-offs in 1894, was the great English innovation, as it remains unknown to baseball.) And between 1991 and 2012, Argentina had a somewhat unusual method of deciding the title, with the country producing two champions per calendar year, the winners of the so-called Apertura and Clausura seasons, respectively. Though the homeland of Maradona and Messi has since switched to a league with one champion a season, this system remains popular in Latin America and some countries, such as Venezuela, then crown an overall champion through a two-legged final between the winners of these tournaments. A bit like baseball's World Series.

Sometimes, the oddities are subtler. This final table in Morocco in 1965–66 is famous as one of the most competitive leagues ever, with only eight points separating the champions from the two relegated clubs.

	P	W	D	L	F	A	Pts
1. Wydad Athletic Club (Casablanca)	26	11	9	6	26	18	57
2. Raja Club Athletic (Casablanca)	26	9	12	5	27	20	56
3. Renaissance Sportive de Settat	26	10	8	8	28	15	54
4. Sporting Club Chabab de Mohammédia	26	8	12	6	19	17	54
5. Kawkab Athletic Club de Marrakech	26	9	9	8	21	21	53
6. TAS (Casablanca)	26	8	10	8	21	20	52
7. Hassania Union Sport Agadir	26	6	14	6	32	33	52
8. Stade Marocain (Rabat)	26	8	9	9	27	27	51
9. Mouloudia Club Oujda	26	5	15	6	27	28	51
10. Racing Athletic Club (Casablanca)	26	7	10	9	17	21	50
11. Maghreb Association Sportive (Fès)	26	6	12	8	13	16	50
12. Fath Union Sport (Rabat)	26	7	10	9	25	31	50
13. Club Omnisport de Meknès	26	7	9	10	16	23	49
14. Maghreb Athletic Tetouan	26	7	9	10	21	30	49

Yet it's also notable because of the points system. Morocco awarded three points for a win (15 years before that was adopted in England and 28 years before it was first used in a World Cup), two for a draw and – oddest of all – one point for a defeat. The innovative idea of rewarding losers has never caught on and Morocco now awards three points for win, one for a draw and nothing for a defeat.

Who invented the long throw?

Not Rory Delap certainly. The devastating monotony with which the Stoke City legend hurtled the ball to the far post so infuriated Arsène Wenger that he proposed FIFA should replace throw-ins with kick-ins or abolish the rule that players can't be offside from a throw-in. If either of Wenger's proposals were adopted, Delap and his fellow practitioners would have to find a new trick and the beautiful game, for which the French coach has appointed himself moral guardian, would be a little less ugly. But Wenger is blaming the wrong man.

If you assess the quality of a long throw purely on distance, the king of the flingers is Dave Challinor who, while on Tranmere's books, threw a record 46.34 metres. But Chelsea fans insist that, in terms of sheer effectiveness, it is hard to beat the great Ian Hutchinson. Hutch's most famous throw, launched into the penalty area at Old Trafford in the 1970 FA Cup final replay, caused such havoc in the Leeds United defence that Dave Webb rose home to head the winner.

Hutch's prowess was exceptional but he was hardly unique. Hennes Weisweiler, who coached the great Borussia Mönchengladbach side of the 1970s, complained in 1978 that: 'Every English team has one player who is expert at the long throw.' Fulham and Spurs certainly did. In the late 1950s and early 1960s, Fulham left-back Jim Langley's ability to wind himself up for throws and launch the ball on to the head of striker Maurice Cook created many goals for the Cottagers. At White Hart Lane, as one Spurs fan noted, 'long throw by Chivers to Alan Gilzean who would flick the ball on with his strangely pyramid-shaped head for Martin Peters to ghost in at the far post to volley home. Worked every time!'

Where some see art, others look for science. In 2006, researchers of Brunei University found that the optimal angle to release the ball for a long throw was 30 degrees. That max-imises height while minimising air resistance. In the summer of 1933, a promising young right-half called Bill Shankly was doing his own experiments. Having just broken into the Carlisle United first team, he returned to his home village Glenbuck for the summer and spent days trying to perfect this tactic, throwing the ball over a row of houses and per-suading local boys to fetch them back for him.

Shankly may have been inspired by Samuel Weaver, a left-half whose throw-ins were said to reach distances of 32m when he was at Hull City in 1928–29. In August 1936, Weaver joined Chelsea and there is a famous photo of him showing off his technique to his new team-mates. They don't

Chelsea's long-throw specialist Sam Weaver could also throw himself over his team-mates. It was unclear what match-winning ploy he had in mind.

look like they're taking the demonstration that seriously. They certainly wouldn't have dreamed that, 34 years later, the club would win the FA Cup with that very technique.

Why do football matches last ninety minutes?

Nobody really knows. The laws of the game did not evolve with Darwinian efficiency. Although Ebenezer Cobb Morley, the first secretary of the FA, published an approved list of the laws of the game on 5 December 1863, those laws did not mention the duration of a game or even specify how many players constituted a team.

In the 1850s and 1860s, Sheffield was the most influential football city in the world. Sheffield FC – the world's oldest club – was formed on 24 October 1857 and a year later, the first laws of the game, known as the Sheffield Rules, were published. These didn't specify how long a game would last or how many players should be on each side either. Adrian Harvey's painstaking history *Football: The First Hundred Years* suggests that Sheffield played with 20 a side and for two hours in the late 1850s. As late as 1862, Harvey says: 'The rules provided no guidance as to the length of time of matches and these could range from anything between one and three hours.'

At this point, the steel city was home to fifteen football clubs and the Sheffield Rules were much more widely used than the Morley/FA rules. The first game we know to have been played over 90 minutes was an inter-city match between Sheffield FC and a team drawn from the London clubs at Battersea Park on 31 March 1866. At the time, the duration of the game seemed less interesting than the Sheffield team's display of aerial prowess which, according to the Sheffield FC website, 'reduced the London players and fans to fits of laughter.' It is certainly possible that the length of that match was dictated by something as prosaic as the duration of the train journey from Sheffield to London. The precedent soon caught on. In 1871, the first rules for the FA Cup stipulated that 'the duration of each match shall be one hour and a half'.

For those who prefer to think the selection of 90 minutes wasn't as arbitrary, Peter Seddon suggests in *Football Talk* that the duration springs from a historic obsession with the number 60 which he dates back to the Middle Ages and the 'division of a clockface into 60 minutes'. Six hundred years ago, Seddon says, 60 represented entirety just as 100 does today. He even suggests that this accounts for the rather arcane scoring system in tennis (15, 30, 40 and game – i.e. 60) if you accept that 40 started as 45 and was shortened on the 'grounds of laziness'. So if, like Seddon, you accept that 'fifteen minute divisions, or multiples thereof, are historically 'tidy'', there might be some logic in the choice of 90 minutes. Certainly, as Seddon points out, coaches often urge their players to keep it tight for the first 15 minutes, the traditional half-time break used to last for 15 minutes and commentators love to crank up the tension by declaring that a game has entered the final 15 minutes.

Indeed Arsène Wenger has even suggested that, 'from a coaching perspective, the key element of the UEFA Champions League is the last ten to fifteen minutes.' The history of European Cup finals bears him out. Eight have been won by decisive goals after the 75th minute and in two others late goals have helped swing the result by setting up extra time.

So football isn't a game of two halves. If Wenger's right, it's a game of six sixths.

⚽ Who first parked the bus?

José Mourinho is credited with first using this term after his Chelsea side had been held to a 0-0 draw by (of all teams) Tottenham at Stamford Bridge in September 2004. The Portuguese coach fumed: 'As they say in Portugal, they brought the bus and they left the bus in front of the goal.' Almost six years later, Mourinho's Inter parked the bus to triumph against Barcelona at the Camp Nou in the semi-final second leg on their way to winning the UEFA Champions League. Two years later, that template came in very handy as Roberto Di Matteo's Chelsea upset the same opponents at the same stage of the competition at the same ground.

Yet Spanish coach Javier Clemente is also famous for using the phrase, promising that his Murcia side would 'park the bus' in front of goal away to Real Madrid in April 2008. Leaving out two strikers, Clemente's Murcia maintained their 7-2-1 formation even after the 19th-minute red card for Real defender Miguel Torres Gómez ... but his side lost 1-0.

Mourinho and Clemente may have coined the term but the tactic is almost as old as the game itself. Helenio Herrera had perfected the defensive art of *catenaccio* in the 1960s, drawing inspiration from – among others – Austrian coach Karl Rappan. In the 1930s, Rappan devised a system to help his semi-professional squad at Servette compete with professionals by minimising the risk of being

The fiendish Helenio Herrera.

caught out in one-on-one encounters. His system, known as *verrou* (the bolt), essentially conceded midfield, encouraging opponents to attack while funnelling their play into the centre of the pitch where they ran into a defensive block moving as a unit. Often criticised as defensive, this system could lead to swift counter-attacks in which six or seven players took part.

In a rare interview, Rappan justified this formation saying: 'The Swiss is not a natural footballer, but he is usually sober in his approach to things. He can be persuaded to think ahead and calculate ahead.' Many coaches, fearing that their players are not naturals, have felt obliged to follow Rappan's example. A few have taken it to extremes. In the 1956 Olympic football tournament, Indonesia held the Soviet Union to a 0-0 draw after their Croatian coach Antun Pogacnik ordered them to keep ten players in their own area whenever they lost possession. They lost the replay 4-0.

⚽ Who was the first playmaker?

You could argue that there is no real godfather to all the classic playmakers that come to mind – from Johan Cruyff or Günter Netzer to Michel Platini, Diego Maradona and Roberto Baggio all the way up to Zinedine Zidane – because the role is almost as old as the game itself. Indeed it was so vital to football that from the 1880s into the 1920s every team contained a playmaker. That's because the pyramid formation so popular in so many countries, the 2-3-5, stood and fell with the man in the middle of what we would now call a three-man midfield: the centre-half.

And yet we would probably not recognise any of the great old centre-halves as a playmaker if we actually saw them play. The reason is as simple as it is surprising – the laws were different. To be precise, the offside laws. Back in the heyday

Arsenal, back in their south London heyday, when the dancing centre-half ruled supreme.

of the original centre-halves – until 1925 – three opposing players (rather than the modern two) were required between the attacker and the goal line when the ball was last played for the striker to be onside. It's hard to visualise the consequences of this rule for a modern fan, so just think about how often a player is offside today following a through ball or a long vertical pass. Now don't multiply this number but square it, and you will quickly understand why back then it was nearly impossible to split a defence or get behind the backline. The pre-1925 game asked for pace and muscle and dribbling skills, not the vision of a playmaker.

Only after that all-important rule change did the modern playmaker begin to emerge, in the 2-3-5 and the new W-M system, usually credited to Arsenal under Herbert Chapman. In this formation, the centre-half became a third back, which meant that the hitherto most creative position became primarily a destructive one. At the same time, the two inside-forwards, previously part of the five-man forward line, were pulled back into a deep-lying position. One of those two would evolve into the team's playmaker, replacing the old attacking centre-half as the main man. It's why Arsenal's Alex James, a star of the 1930s, has often been called the first modern playmaker. Just listen to Brian Glanville, who enthused that 'his beautifully judged and powerfully struck passes from midfield, some through the middle to a charging, challenging centre-forward, some inside the full-back to Bastin, on the left wing, some across field to the racing Joe Hulme, were of priceless effect'.

There were other notable string-pullers like James during this decade. Sunderland's Raich Carter, for instance (whom Sir Stanley Matthews called 'bewilderingly clever, constructive, lethal in front of goal, yet unselfish'). Or the brilliant Argentine Antonio Sastre, who orchestrated Independiente's play in the 1930s.

All of these great players, and others, have been hailed as the inventor of the playmaking role but to find the true originator you must go back further still. The offside rule changed in 1925 but James only emerged as Arsenal's key man in 1929. Two players filled the role of the scheming, withdrawn inside-forward in Chapman's system before James. His immediate predecessor was Charlie Buchan. He had suggested the W-M in the first place, had always wanted to be the deep-lying link man and filled that role until he retired in 1928. But when Chapman introduced the new system, he didn't use Buchan as link man, turning instead to the veteran Andrew Neil, about whom he noted, 'he is slow as a funeral but has ball control'.

Yet it's not simply the position that maketh the playmaker. As good as Neil and Buchan may have been, they weren't compared to an orchestra's conductor, nor did the country's intelligentsia write poems about them. Unlike the legendary Austrian Matthias Sindelar. In the 1920s, the Danubian school stuck to the 2-3-5, so you'd expect Sindelar to have filled the old centre-half role, the more so since he was lightweight, pencil-thin and disliked any form of bodily contact (all of which explains why they called him the Paper Man). But he was the centre-forward. With a twist.

Matthias Sindelar, the Paper Man, became a legend in Austria after refusing to give the Nazi salute to Hitler after the *Anschluss*.

Like the Hungarian Nándor Hidegkuti in the 1950s or Johan Cruyff in the 1970s, Sindelar was a centre-forward who loved to drop back, exchange passes with a midfielder (in the national team, this was centre-half Josef 'Pepi' Smistik) and then distribute the ball or make runs himself. He had technique, vision and style. Maybe too much style. He made his Austria debut in 1926, at 23, but fell foul of national coach Hugo Meisl two years later after his playfulness lost the team a game played on a slippery, snowy surface. Stubborn, like all great playmakers, Sindelar refused to cut down on his elegant dribbles or beloved short passes and gave away the ball so often on that cold afternoon that Meisl lost patience.

Yet fans and writers demanded Sindelar's return and Meisl finally relented in time for a game against Scotland in May 1931. Austria sensationally won 5-0. It was the birth of a side known as the Wunderteam – and Sindelar was its brains. The drama critic and essayist Alfred Polgar put it this way: 'He would play football as a grandmaster plays chess: with a broad mental conception, calculating moves and countermoves in advance, always choosing the most promising of all possibilities.' And the writer Friedrich Torberg composed a poem which said that 'he played nonchalantly, delicately, cheerfully – he always played, he never fought'. Which is as good a description of the classic playmaker as you're likely to read.

But Sindelar was not just a footballer. In 1938, after Nazi Germany annexed Austria, Sindelar led Austria to victory in a celebratory game between the two nations, pointedly refusing (along with fellow scorer Karl Sesta) to make a Nazi salute to Hitler beforehand. He then refused to play for a united German team. In 1939, he was found dead, probably due to carbon monoxide poisioning, though Gestapo involvement was strongly suspected. His club, Austria Vienna, received 15,000 telegrams of condolence.

⚽ Who was the first sweeper-keeper?

'**Go out and make mistakes.**' That's what Ajax coach Johan Cruyff told his young keeper Stanley Menzo in 1985–86. A brilliant shot-stopper, Menzo was usually adept at clearing up behind the defence but sometimes took his coach's advice too literally. Two blunders by Menzo against Auxerre in 1993 – under Cruyff's successor Louis van Gaal – smoothed the way for Edwin van der Sar to perfect the sweeper-keeper role.

This style of goalkeeping had been influential in Dutch football ever since the 1970s. Selecting his 1974 World Cup squad, Netherlands coach Rinus Michels decided that Jan Jongbloed's ability to operate as an extra defender, playing 20 yards from his goal with his feet, was more useful than the agile, shot-stopping of Jan van Beveren. Jongbloed's brief wasn't that sophisticated: he usually had to get the ball first and kick it into touch but Van der Sar became the pivot of Ajax's rapid 'circulation football', a style Van Gaal exported to Barcelona, laying the foundations for tiki-taka. As Chris Keulemans, an amateur goalkeeper and Dutch novelist, told David Winner, 'some goalkeepers regard the ball as their enemy because it is trying to penetrate their sacred area, but Van der Sar regards it as his friend.'

In the 1990s, Van der Sar, Peter Schmeichel and the gifted, but erratic, Fabien Barthez emerged as gifted sweeper-keepers. Today, the best exponent of that role is probably Barcelona's Víctor Valdés. But they weren't the first players in that position to regard the ball as a friend. Before the 1990 World Cup, Colombia coach Francisco Maturana put his faith in René Higuita who, he wrote, 'gives us something no one else has. With René as sweeper, we have eleven outfield players'.

In hindsight, Higuita's career has been telescoped into one scorpion kick and one famous failure to sweep up that let Roger Milla score for Cameroon at Italia 90. At the very moment Higuita lost the ball near his own halfway line, the Colombian TV commentator was describing him as 'an exceptional sweeper'.

From such highlights, the legend of Higuita as El Loco was born. In fairness, Higuita's self-confidence had often provided the inspiration for an exceptional Colombian side. In 1988, in a friendly against England at Wembley, the keeper dribbled around Gary Lineker as if, in Maturana's words, 'it was a game in the park back home'.

Maturana had looked back to Jongbloed for inspiration. But Michels, who had selected Jongbloed, was looking back even further – to the great Hungarian side of 1953 and their keeper Gyula Grosics. Under their innovative coach Gusztáv Sebes, Hungary's shift in tactics to a 4-2-4 with a withdrawn striker created, as Grosics recalled, 'an attacking game-plan that provided more opportunities for the opposition to counter-attack when they got possession. There was space behind our defence to be exploited and I had to act as a kind of extra sweeper, outside my area, trying to reach the through ball before the opponent did.' With a looser back four, Grosics learned to roll the ball out because it was more accurate, and quicker, than just kicking it up the pitch. This tactic was so successful that Ferenc Puskás and Nándor Hidegkuti would drop back to pick up a throw. The success of this approach impressed Michels, then a no-thrills centre-forward for Ajax, who would use the same ploy when he became the Amsterdammers' coach.

Of course, there is also an entirely different way for a goalkeeper to 'exploit space' – he could, like Franz Beckenbauer would one day, run into it with the ball at his feet. In fact, there was a keeper known for precisely such suicidal forays deep, deep into the opponents' half long before the Kaiser

Put your hands in the air for the original sweeper-keeper, the man in black, 1860 Munich's Petar Radenkovíc.

invented the attacking sweeper. And since this goalkeeper was playing in Munich, it is tempting to rewrite history and say it wasn't Giacinto Facchetti's runs down the wing that inspired Beckenbauer but a batty Yugoslav we have met before – 1860 Munich's Petar Radenković.

Radenković, who'd won three caps in the 1950s, became the Bundesliga's first foreign superstar during the league's inaugural season, 1963–64, in part because the nation finally saw what 1860's fans had already become used to: Radenković's spectacular solo runs. Like Grosics, the Yugoslav would roll the ball out, or rather: pretend to. Because if there was no opponent in the vicinity, Radenković would roll the ball into his own path – and run. His solos could literally take him as far as the other team's penalty area and he was so fearless – or reckless – that he would make them even on snowy, slippery surfaces.

This combination of eccentricity and showmanship ran in the family (see 'What was the top pop hit by a footballer', p.260). However, Radenković maintains: 'My runs had nothing to do with putting on a show. I was just creating modern goalkeeping. I had been an outfield player during my youth, and I learned that you don't just hoof the ball away.'

⚽ Who invented the stepover?

The global popularity of a trick that Cristiano Ronaldo turned into his signature move is reflected in the variety of terms used to describe it. In German-speaking countries, the stepover is sometimes called the *Scherentrick*, literally scissor trick, but more commonly known as an *übersteiger*, a climb over. In France, they call it, rather poetically, *un passement des jambes* (a passing of the legs), while the Italians, as if the trick was performed on the dance floor, call it *un doppio passo* (a double step) and the Spanish, confusingly, refer to it as *la bicicleta* (which they also use to describe a bicycle kick).

This profusion of terms reflects the complex roots of this showboaters' trademark. Apart from CR7, most of the famous recent exponents have been Brazilian. The Brazilian Ronaldo famously used his shuffle to win the 1998 UEFA Cup for Inter, prompting an awestruck Kevin Keegan to say: 'We've all seen those skills before – but not at 100mph.' Denilson's exuberant use of the trick prompted British rapper JME (or grime artist if we're being absolutely accurate) to cut a track in 2009 called 'Over Me' which includes the line 'I'm quick, like Denilson stepover'. And in Chile, Club de Deportes La Serena star Eduardo Rubio, is nicknamed *El Bicicleta*, the Stepover. He has also been dubbed the triathlete, because he '*corre, bicicleta y nada*' –

runs, bicycles, and *nada* – which means both 'swims' and 'nothing' in Spanish.

So the obvious place to look to trace the evolution of the stepover might seem to be South America. But to do that would be to ignore the contributions made by two of Gazza's best mates, a German midfielder nicknamed after asparagus, and a tragic Dutch speed skating aficionado.

Let's start in the not too distant past with Gazza's former mentor, Glenn Roeder. In the 1980s, Newcastle United's languid central defender used the stepover to get out of trouble. He did this so often – sometimes twice on the same opponent – that it was called the Glenn Roeder shuffle. When asked to explain the origins of this move, Roeder said his dad taught him it 'many moons ago'.

'Go across the ball with the outside of the right or left foot, feint with the upper part of the body and cut inside.' Cristiano Ronaldo prepares to roll.

Roeder was hardly the only player to realise the fun that could be had by stepping over the ball. The same thought had occurred, to mention just a few names, to Francesco Totti, Luís Figo, Robinho, Zinedine Zidane and Chris Waddle. In his prime at Marseille, Waddle, Gazza's long-suffering former room-mate, liked to deceive defenders by doing the stepover at jogging pace or at a standstill, lazily jabbing his foot over the ball before he dropped his shoulder and accelerated away.

For fans in Germany and the Netherlands, such artistry was impressive but hardly new. In the 1970s, this sleight of foot was the making of Hans 'Hannes' Bongartz, the great Schalke midfielder nicknamed Asparagus Tarzan (the plant is often used to describe long-legged German footballers). It led to him being lauded, in one club history, as the inventor of the stepover. Was he? Alas, no – not even in Germany. Earlier in the decade, coach Karl-Heinz Heddergott had published a book called *Neue Fussball Lehre* (New Football Teaching) in which the move – referred to as the *Scherentrick* (scissor trick) is described in detail. The book instructs players: 'Go across the ball with the outside of the right or left foot, feint with the upper part of the body and cut inside.'

Ajax's reclusive legend Piet Keizer had no need of such instructions. Dutch coach Bert van Marwijk recalled watching Keizer and copying his moves, saying, 'Piet was more Mr Stepover like Ronaldo.' But where did Keizer get the idea? Possibly from watching Abe Lenstra, the tricky left-sided player who won 47 Dutch caps between 1940 and 1959 and would have won many more if he hadn't insisted the selectors play him in his preferred inside-forward position. There is a YouTube clip of Lenstra rehearsing his stepover on the training ground.

Lenstra may have been perfecting the manoeuvre at around the same period as Chilean left-half Augusto 'The Kid' Arenas was insisting he had invented it. The left-half, who won the Chilean title with Everton de Viña del Mar in 1952, was determined that no one else would get the credit, saying: 'The stepover is mine, all who saw me know that.' Yet other remarks made by Arenas suggest we shouldn't take his assertion at face value. The left-half told the newspaper *La Cuarta*: 'This is nothing – several times I dived from the top of the cranes on the Vergara pier, I was featherweight champion, played basketball – and gave mambo dancing classes.'

Arenas' bombast would be disputed by fans of forward Jair da Rosa Pinto, who was credited, in his native Brazil, with inventing the move. Yet by a tragic quirk of football history, the claims of Master Jaja – as he was known – have largely been overlooked. His career – indeed his life – never recovered from his participation in the de facto final of the 1950 World Cup which Brazil, as hosts and favourites, catastrophically lost 2-1 to Uruguay.

Yet as far back as the 1930s, Italy's World Cup-winning midfielder Amedeo Biavati was thrilling crowds, and *Azzurri* coach Vittorio Pozzo, with this same technique. At the time Pozzo said: 'Biavati perfected the stepover. The public expected it every time he took off down the touchline. And the opponent expected it too. But there was nothing he could do. At full speed Amedeo executed a kind of little jump in the air, it seemed as if he was going to do a back heel. The defender slowed down for an instant, Biavati surged past him, touching the ball with his second foot and was off.' Such feints inspired a young Bologna supporter called Pier Paolo Pasolini who said later: 'When I played, I said "I am Biavati".'

The film director's idol was one of the first players to make the stepover famous. But he was not the first. A fragile genius from the Dutch East Indies (as Indonesia was then known) called Law Adam had already perfected this trick. In October 1932, the Dutch newspaper *Het Vaderland* covered a friendly between the Netherlands and Belgium in Brussels. With 15 minutes to go, and the score at 2-2, Adam slipped past one opponent and then beat Belgian skipper Nicolas Hooydonckx with a trick the paper refers to as his *bekende schaarbeweging* (well-known scissor move). The paper's description suggests the stepover may have been Adam's signature move, and contemporary accounts suggest he got the idea from watching speed skaters. Speed skating over frozen canals, often over long distances, was then a popular Dutch pastime. Speed skaters make these stepover movements and do so in such a way that it's easy to see why this trick might be dubbed the scissor move.

Adam might be more famous had he not suffered from a heart condition which forced him to retire at the age of 25, in 1933, and killed him on 15 May 1941. His final hours read like a scene in a Victorian adventure novel. Back in Asia, he was playing a friendly in Surbaya, his home town. After two goals and three assists, he left the pitch in the 53rd minute with his hand on his heart. He assured the referee it wasn't serious, that he was leaving because victory was assured, but within an hour he was pronounced dead. Still, the legend of Adam's scissor move still resonates in Dutch popular culture. In 1974, the Dutch author Jan Wolkers published a novel called *De Walgvogel*. In the first chapter – entitled 'Adam de Schaarman' (Adam The Scissors Man) – the first-person narrator describes his uncle's attempt to perfect the move.

Spoiler alert. This is Pedro Calomino – the man who invented the stepover.

Adam may have introduced the stepover to Europe but even he didn't invent it. The balance of evidence suggests that the man who first perfected this move was Argentinian footballer Pedro Calomino. Authoritative claims that the Boca Juniors legend invented the stepover can be traced back as far as 1910. In *Soccer vs. The State: Tackling Football And Radical Politics*, Gabriel Kuhn says Calomino was one of the stars of Boca's first golden age: 'Spectators no longer came just to watch their teams – they came to watch their idols. One of them was Pedro Calomino, cheered on by the Boca fans in Genovese Spanish: "*Idaguele Calumín, dáguele!*" ("Do it, Calumín, do it!"). Calomino was always oblivious to the stands. He stood on the field, waited for the ball and made defenders dizzy with his incredible dribbles. He was the inventor of the *bicicleta*, the stepover.'

One reason Calomino was so popular was that he seemed to embody the club. The influence of Genovese immigrants in Boca's early history was so profound that even today the club is still nicknamed Xeneize (Genovese). Calomino's family were Genovese and he painted boats to support his family before becoming a footballer. He was an old-fashioned winger, so old-fashioned he didn't like to wear boots. Boca got permission for him to play wearing espadrilles. None of this prevented him from destroying opponents with his stepover. Fairly reliable sources tell of a game between Argentina and a Basque XI in which defender Arrate, tiring of the Boca star's tricks, told him: 'You can go forwards, you can play backwards, but just play with good faith.'

Calomino won four league titles at Boca, scored 82 goals in 182 games there (he was top scorer for six seasons) and starred in the Argentine side that won the 1921 Copa America. He retired in 1924, aged 32, because he had trouble with his right eye. But he remains a legend at Boca where he invented the stepover at their stadium.

That trick continues to delight fans and footballers – even amateurs. Reggae legend Bob Marley was so passionate about football he insisted on having access to a pitch on his world tours. A skilful midfield general – with a hard man called Skully acting as a kind of security guard on the pitch – Bob can be seen doing a stepover in the 2012 documentary film, *Marley*.

⚽ Who invented **Total Football**?

The usual answer – Rinus Michels' Ajax – is not necessarily right. In the early 1970s, Michels' Ajax, led by the paradigm shifting genius of Johan Cruyff, thrilled and conquered Europe with a stylish brand of football in which every outfield player could play in any position. But they didn't entirely invent it.

Tactical guru Jonathan Wilson argues that the innovative Russian coach Viktor Maslov (see 'Who invented 4-4-2?', p.8) had laid the basis for such fluidity, introducing the pressing game at Dynamo Kiev in the 1960s. You could only pressure the ball if you were absolutely confident a team-mate would

Rinus Michels – a man synonymous with Total Football – explains how he wants everyone to play. But did he learn it all from Leicester City?

cover for you and that could only happen if every player could see beyond their own specialist role and read the game.

Affectionately known to his players as Grandad, Maslov started coaching Kiev in 1964. Dynamo midfielder Yozhef Szabo says in Jonathan Wilson's book *Inverting The Pyramid*: 'In the course of the game there was complete interchangeability. This team developed the prototype of Total Football. People think it was invented in Holland but that is just because, in western Europe, they didn't see Maslov's Dynamo.' Or as Valeriy Lobanovskiy, another great Dynamo coach, who played under Maslov, put it: 'There is no such thing as a striker, a midfielder, a defender. There are only footballers and they should be able to do everything on the pitch.' To make his point, Lobanovskiy would make his players wear blindfolds in five-a-side games.

Yet – somewhat bizarrely – one year before Maslov even took charge at Kiev – and eight years before Ajax won their first European Cup at Wembley – a variant of Total Football was already being played by Matt Gillies' Leicester City, who reached the 1963 FA Cup final, losing 3-1 to Matt Busby's Manchester United. Football historians who have an instinctive preference for setting every tactical innovation in a wider, socio-political context might baulk at this suggestion. There is a kind of cultural snobbery at work which makes it easier to imagine revolutionary new tactics being honed in the glamorous fervent of 1960s Amsterdam or in the pseudo-scientific, quasi-academic world of Soviet sport than on a training pitch in the East Midlands.

Or at a very unfashionable club in the heart of West Germany's decidedly unglamorous Ruhr region. Because at the same time that Leicester stunned England, a Meidericher SV (now MSV Duisburg) team assembled on a shoestring budget shocked the Bundesliga by finishing as runners-up in 1963–64. The secret of their success was a tactical system their coach had improvised to suit his players. The coach was Rudi Gutendorf (see 'Who has coached the most national teams?') and his strategy became known as *der Riegel*, the bolt. This name, and the fact that Meidericher SV were hardly a superpower, led many to presume that Gutendorf's game was ultra-defensive. In a way, it was – because everybody defended. But at the same time, and this has been forgotten, almost everybody attacked.

Gutendorf's system was dubbed *der Riegel* because the whole team would move forward and backwards, like a bolt. While most teams were playing the W-M system, Meiderich used only two men up front, being cautious but also giving those attackers more room in which to operate. Their job was to pull defenders out of position and open up space for attacking full-backs. In November 1964, the noted magazine *Der Spiegel* said: 'Meiderich defended with attackers and attacked with defenders.' (It also quoted national coach Sepp Herberger as saying: 'This is modern football.' He might as well have said: 'This is Total Football.')

The new system didn't catch on because it demanded too much of players steeped in a simpler game. Even though Meiderich finished second, captain Werner Krämer approached Gutendorf in pre-season training and told him the team was unhappy because all the running up and down the pitch was wearing them out.

Leicester's players were more obedient. In the 1963 FA Cup Final programme *Sunday Mirror* journalist Sam Leitch has this to say of City's style: 'Millions of words have sought to explain the successful formula of the Leicester play. Tactics, that mysterious seven-letter word that is so easy to write but more difficult to explain, has been behind it all. Gillies is the first to admit football is a simple game but it can be changed around. Why should the number of players' shirts shackle them to a fixed role? If eight men can attack, why cannot eight defend?'

The Leicester manager was a tactical pioneer in a period of British football when, he said, 'players hadn't gone beyond thinking about numbers'. A ploy as simple as swapping right-half Frank McLintock and inside-right Graham Cross was enough to confound many opponents.

Inspired by the great Austria and Hungary teams of the 1950s, Gillies had Leicester playing a patient, possession-based game relying on short, probing passes and the flexible, position-swapping play of wing-halves, inside-forwards and wingers. While Cross and McLintock interchanged on the right, tireless winger Mike Stringfellow and playmaking inside-forward Davie Gibson swapped on the left. Defenders never knew if Gibson was going to feed Stringfellow or drift out wide and play a sharp, angled pass into the box for converted centre-forward Ken Keyworth to exploit.

Such tactics were startling – and successful – enough to take Leicester to two FA Cup finals in three years (they also lost in 1961 to Bill Nicholson's double-winning Spurs) and fourth place in the old First Division in 1962–63. They also inspired Bill Shankly who soon ordered Liverpool's Gordon Milne and Tommy Smith to swap places, like Cross and McLintock.

Gillies was a trailblazer, not the inventor. Like Michels, he had been inspired by the free-flowing style of Gusztav Sebes' great Hungarian side illuminated by the talents of Ferenc Puskás, Nandor Hidegkuti, Zoltan Czibor and Jozsef Bozsik. But even Sebes didn't invent Total Football. In the 1930s, the Austrian Wunderteam, under Hugo Meisl, played with such improvisational genius that opponents were stupefied. In 1955, Hugo's younger brother Willy wrote a classic book called *Soccer Revolution* in which he dubbed this system 'The Whirl'. In the book, he demanded: 'We must free our soccer

Hugo Meisl's Austrian Wunderteam take to the field in the 1930s – the painting is by Paul Meissner. Sindelar is fourth from right. Meisl has the hat and cane.

youth from playing to order, along rails, as it were.' He also suggested, a decade before Michels started coaching at Ajax: 'Every man-jack must be able to tackle anybody else's job temporarily without any ado.'

Meisl's Wunderteam wouldn't have been as dazzling without the great, unpredictable genius of Matthias Sindelar (see 'Who was the first playmaker?'). Austrian football writer Friedrich Torberg said of Sindelar: 'He had no system nor set pattern. He just had … genius.'

And therein lies some of the difficulty in tracing the tortuous history of Total Football. Traditionally, this philosophy's development is described almost exclusively in terms of coaches, tactics and systems, yet the quality of the players was crucial. Instead of a Sindelar or a Cruyff, Leicester manager Gillies had Gibson and McLintock – gifted players but hardly the icons to inspire a revolution. As innovative as Gillies' tactics were, the Foxes won more plaudits than silverware – even with Gordon Banks in goal. The Scot won the League Cup in 1964, suffered tuberculosis and left Filbert Street in November 1968. Six months later, City lost their third FA Cup final in nine years and were relegated.

As visionary as Michels was, he inherited – rather than invented – the genius of Cruyff. And it was free-thinkers like Cruyff, Franz Beckenbauer has suggested, who were at the heart of that football revolution. 'It owed more to the element of surprise than any magic formula,' said the Kaiser. 'The Dutch got away with it so long because the opposition could never work out what tactics they were facing. There were no tactics at all. Just brilliant players with a ball.'

Oddities

🌑 Do you always have to wear boots to play football?

You do now – since FIFA changed the laws. The team that most famously fell foul of the custom of wearing boots was India's 1950 World Cup side that missed the tournament because they wanted to play barefoot. Except, as you will discover, the story is a bit more complicated than that.

First, whenever this anecdote is retold, people assume that India was a backward football nation at the time. That was not quite the case. Delhi's annual Durand Cup is the third oldest football competition – after England's FA Cup and the Scottish Cup. But it is true that the Indian FA joined FIFA in 1948 partly so the national team could compete in that year's

London Olympics and it is true that field hockey, not football, was – and is – India's national sport.

Some of the best Indian footballers started out playing hockey or represented their country at both games. In India, hockey was often played barefoot. Not because the players couldn't afford shoes, but because they found it easier and more comfortable to play that way. In the final of the 1936 Olympic hockey tournament, India played in shoes and were losing at half-time (to hosts Germany). After star player Dhyan Chand took off his shoes, India won 8-1.

When India sent a football team to the 1948 Olympics, contrary to popular myth, the players were neither bad (they only lost 2-1 to France after missing two penalties) and didn't all play barefoot. Many did, because they were used to it from hockey – and at the time, this wasn't officially forbidden – though 'barefoot' is perhaps a misleading term. Those players who didn't have boots protected their feet with bandages.

Two years later, India qualified for the 1950 World Cup without playing a game, as their three qualifying opponents – Burma, Indonesia and the Philippines – all withdrew at the eleventh hour. Many countries, in fact, didn't bother with the 1950 World Cup in Brazil. Austria, Belgium, Finland and France all declined to take part due to the expensive, arduous travel involved. Which is why FIFA were so keen for India to play they even offered to pay for the flights to Brazil. But the Indian FA kept making new demands – until finally they asked for an exemption from a new rule, the one that said players had to wear boots. FIFA refused, India stayed home.

The truly strange thing about this saga is that the Indian FA didn't consult their players. Most of them would have happily played in boots in Brazil. Indeed, the whole team wore boots at the 1956 Melbourne Olympics. For that tournament,

The Indian team training barefoot for the 1948 Olympics.

they asked the organisers if players could take them off if the boots' weight caused cramps but – boots or no boots – India's team came fourth, winning a quarter-final 4-2 against hosts Australia. Coach Syed Abdul Rahim, a student of Hungary's free-flowing Magical Magyars, played Samar Banerjee as a withdrawn centre-forward, a revolutionary tactic that flummoxed opponents. The affronted Australians demanded a rematch after the Olympics (which they lost 7-1).

The most likely, though no less mysterious, explanation for India's failure to compete in the 1950 World Cup is that the Indian FA had absolutely no interest in sending a team to this or any other tournament. Because four years later, ahead of the 1954 finals, they sent in their registration only after the deadline for doing so had expired. After that, FIFA would not hear anything from Delhi for three decades. Which is why India played its first-ever World Cup qualifier on 21 March 1985, losing 2-1 to Indonesia. Krishanu Dey, an attacking midfielder revered as the Indian Maradona, scored his country's first goal in the history of the competition.

🌑 Who was the first player to wear coloured boots?

In October 1973, Bayern Munich needed a shoot-out to edge past Swedish champions Åtvidaberg in the first round of the European Cup. Conny Torstensson had stood out for the Swedes – because he scored twice in the second leg and because of his footwear. Wilhelm Neudecker, who was Bayern's president, said: 'I want the striker with the red boots' and the club soon signed him.

Torstensson's red boots were distinctive but not historic. Four years before, Alan Ball had worn white boots for Everton in the Charity Shield. Yet these boots weren't quite what they seemed. As Brian Hewitt, who was marketing director for Hummel Football Boots recalled, 'When the boots were first introduced to the UK, I made them white to make them stand out from adidas and Puma. But while Hummel did make boots, Alan couldn't initially wear them so we actually had his adidas boots painted white and delivered them to him ten minutes before the start of the game.'

Before Ball's flamboyant gesture, boots had traditionally been black or brown. Yet sixty or so years before Hummel got the paint brushes out, a tubby striker called Herbert Chapman had decided that bright yellow boots would make it easier for his team-mates to spot him. The stats suggest they also made it simpler for defenders to mark him. In one prolific spell at Northampton Town, Chapman scored 14 goals in 22 games but his strike rate at Spurs – 16 goals in 42 games between 1905 and 1907 – was more representative of his career as a whole.

Chapman's flamboyance was a harbinger of an age where, despite the grumbling of such old school coaches as Martin O'Neill, black boots have become the exception rather than the norm. Football boots is one branch of the fashion business where the hot trendy thing – the new black if you will – will never be black.

Alan Ball white boots: every English schoolboy's dream, c.1967, along with George Best's purple-and-black Stylo Matchmakers.

🌍 What was the most brutal game of football ever?

Traditionally, the South Americans are the specialists – and indeed they were involved in all three World Cup matches that are quasi-officially designated battles: the Battle of Bordeaux (1938), the Battle of Berne (1954) and the Battle of Santiago (1962). But Italians and Glaswegians have played significant supporting roles.

Bordeaux actually seems more of a skirmish compared to the mayhem of the following two. A 1-1 draw between Brazil and Czechoslovakia was marred by three sending offs (Machado and Zezé Procópio for Brazil; Jan Riha for the Czechoslovaks), while Oldrich Nejedly suffered a broken leg, captain Frantisek Planicka's right arm was broken and Josef Kostalek was injured in the stomach. The carnage was completed by injuries to the tournament's top goalscorer Leonidas and Brazilian striker José Perácio.

Sixteen years later, Brazil were embroiled in an even more violent tussle with Hungary. The tone was set in the third minute when Hidegkuti gave Hungary the lead only to have his shorts ripped off as he scored. Both sides conceded penalties with rash defending but referee Arthur Ellis, later renowned for his benign officiating on *It's A Knockout*, had to send off Bozsik and Nilton Santos for fighting, and then young Brazilian left-back Humberto Tozzi for kicking Gyula Lóránt. Scoring the winner to make it 3-2 must have been especially thrilling for Zoltán Czibor given that, as Brian Glanville notes in his *The Story Of The World Cup*, 'he had been chased around the field by an incensed and threatening Djalma Santos'.

The violence escalated as the match ended. Someone – some witnesses say it was Puskás, though he denied it – threw a bottle at the Brazilian centre-half. Enraged, the Brazilians invaded the Hungarian dressing room, leaving coach Sebes needing four stitches after the confrontation. Brazilian fans spat on Ellis's car as he left the stadium. The official's verdict on the match? 'Whether it was politics or religion I don't know but they behaved like animals.'

Another Englishman, commentator David Coleman, would be even more eloquent about the Battle of Santiago in 1962. He introduced the BBC's coverage of the match between hosts Chile and Italy with these unforgettable remarks: 'Good evening. The game you are about to see is the most stupid, appalling, disgusting and disgraceful exhibition of football possibly in the history of the game.'

English referee Ken Aston sends off Italian player Mario David, as an injured Chilean lies on the ground, during the World Cup clash at Santiago, 1962.

Coleman wasn't exaggerating. The game started with the Chilean players spitting at their opponents and the eighth-minute sending off of *Azzurri* midfielder Giorgio Ferrini. It took eight minutes – and police intervention – for Ferrini to leave the pitch. Chilean midfielder Leonel Sánchez responded to a series of kicks from Italian defender Mario David by flattening him. When British referee Ken Aston gave no foul, David took matters into his own hands, or feet, and was sent off for kicking the midfielder in the neck. Sánchez celebrated by breaking Italian forward Humberto Maschio's nose with a left-hook his dad, a professional boxer, would have been proud of. The linesman ignored the punch so Sánchez stayed on.

Aston later complained that he wasn't 'reffing a football match, I was acting as an umpire in military manoeuvres'. The Italians insisted the English referee had been bought. In reality, he had just reacted incompetently as the game descended into violence, though he did give every significant decision to the home side as Chile won 2-0.

As grim as all that sounds, it's nothing compared to the violent mayhem that made the play-off to decide the 1967 Intercontinental Cup memorable for all the wrong reasons. Before the second leg in Buenos Aires, Celtic keeper Ronnie Simpson had been knocked out cold by a stone hurled from the stand and with Jimmy Johnstone kicked around the pitch with impunity, Racing Club won 2-1 to tie the series and necessitate a play-off in Montevideo. The game was so dramatic that trying to reconstruct who did what to whom and why they were sent off is extremely difficult. After 25 minutes, Paraguayan referee Rodolfo Perez Oserio was so alarmed by the way the game was being played, he called the captains together and warned them. It had little effect.

When Johnstone was chopped down for the umpteenth time, he retaliated. Racing defender Alfio Basile (who later coached Argentina) spat at Celtic winger Bobby Lennox and, after the predictable mass pugilism, both players were sent off (although Basile had actually been fighting with John Clark and Lennox was far away when the offence was committed). Racing keeper Agustín Cejas admitted later that Basile's foul on John-stone was 'one of the most violent I've ever seen', but that didn't stop him walking up to his injured opponent and 'kicking him as hard as I could for getting my team-mate sent off'.

At half-time, Johnstone had to wash opponents' spit out of his hair. Three minutes into the second half, 'Jinky' was dismissed for the crime of being rugby tackled by Racing defender Oscar Martin. French journalist Francis Thébaud, covering the match for *Miroir du Football*, looked on incredu-lously: 'He who had been the constant target of the aggression since the beginning of the match became the victim of the man who was supposed to protect the footballer against the fakers and foulers. It was a staggering decision.'

Among all the carnage, Racing striker José Cardenas found time to score the only goal and Tommy Gemmell seized the opportunity to kick an opponent up the backside. All that remained was for Celtic forward John Hughes to be sent off after a foul on Racing keeper Cejas and for Rulli to be dismissed too, for a relatively mild offence. Two minutes later, after another free-for-all, Oserio seemed to send off Bertie Auld but the headstrong Celtic midfielder refused to leave the pitch.

After six sendings off (even though Auld didn't leave) and 51 fouls, the finale to the play-off was grimly appropriate. Racing's attempted lap of honour was curtailed as they were pelted with whatever the Uruguayans in the crowd could find to throw at them. The Argentinian paper *La Racon* crowed: 'Racing have recovered the glory days.' The *Miroir du Football* had a different take in its headline: 'Racing: Champions of the world of violence, treachery and theatrics.' Celtic directors were so appalled they fined their players £250 each. If you've ever wondered why Jock Stein never got his knighthood, this might be the reason.

Needless to say, there is some terrific footage of all these battles on YouTube.

⚫ Who were the most careless owners of a trophy?

Sometimes you wonder why athletes invest so much time and effort trying to win a trophy, when they often seem to lose all respect for the object of desire once it's theirs. The tragi-comic history of carelessness starts with the very first football trophy – the original FA Cup was stolen in 1895 from a Birmingham shop window, where winners Aston Villa had put it on display, and was never recovered.

Yet the English obviously didn't learn from the experience, as 71 years later, while staging the World Cup, they allowed the Jules Rimet Trophy to be nicked while on display at Westminster Central Hall. Luckily, the cup was found a week later by Pickles, a black and white collie dog. (Fearful of a repeat, the FA secretly commissioned a replica of the trophy. It's this replica that Bobby Moore holds aloft in English football's most iconic image.)

Alas, dog and trophy suffered sad fates. Pickles became famous enough to have the same agent as Spike Milligan but, after a brief appearance in the British comedy *The Spy With A Cold Nose*, strangled himself on his lead while chasing a cat in 1967. And in December 1983, the real Jules Rimet Trophy was stolen again, from the headquarters of the Brazilian FA in Rio. No dog came to the rescue so the Jules Rimet is not still gleaming – as the David Baddiel and Frank Skinner lyrics

Pickles the collie being interviewed at the crime scene where he discovered the World Cup trophy, discarded in a ditch.

to 'Three Lions (Football's Coming Home)' might suggest – having almost certainly been melted down by the thieves.

Club sides don't treat their trophies much better. The Germans are almost as careless as the English. In 1978, Magdeburg won the East German FA Cup for the fifth time and were allowed to keep it. In 1990, it disappeared. Just like that. Maybe it was stolen, maybe not – it's just not there anymore. In 2002, in a reunified Germany, Schalke paraded the cup in triumph through their home town Gelsenkirchen only for the trophy to slip from the grasp of business manager Rudi Assauer and loop on to the asphalt. The club brought the badly damaged cup to Wilhelm Nagel, the Cologne goldsmith who had created the modern trophy in 1964. 'The first time I saw it, tears welled up in my eyes,' Nagel said. The then 75-year-old worked for five months until he had restored the cup to its former glory. (Assauer paid the £21,000 bill for repairs.)

Careless hands struck again in April 2011, when Real Madrid paraded the Copa del Rey, which they hadn't won in 18 years. Dropped by defender Sergio Ramos, the trophy was crushed under the bus's front right wheel. Only a few weeks later, Dutch side Ajax rode through Amsterdam to present the Eredivisie trophy to their fans. Goalkeeper Maarten Stekelenburg, of all people, dropped the silver plate and watched it bounce along the road. A year later, Ajax dropped the trophy again. This time defender Jan Vertonghen let it fall on to his left foot after Ajax had clinched the title. The trophy was undamaged but Vertonghen's sock was left soaked with blood.

That same month the *Daily Mail* reported that 'three members of Chelsea's staff have been suspended after the Champions League trophy was damaged'. The newspaper explained: 'One of the handles was left hanging off after the three security personnel posed for pictures with the trophy to show off to friends.'

Posing for pictures, as Aston Villa can testify, is often where the trouble starts. In May 1982, when the Villains won the European Cup, left-back Colin Gibson and midfielder Gordon Cowans were tasked with bringing it back from Rotterdam. In celebratory mood, they took the gigantic silverware to the Fox Inn near Tamworth. After a few photos, and a few drinks, the players began a darts match until, at some point, Gibson recalls, 'someone turned around and said the cup's been stolen'. Luckily, it turned up – 100 miles away at West Bar police station in the centre of Sheffield. Before their colleagues from the West Midlands arrived to retrieve the trophy, the younger police on duty at West Bar played in full uniform for the honour of 'winning' the European Cup. What the police in Sheffield and the West Midlands still don't know, more than 30 years later, is who stole the trophy, why and how it came to end up in Sheffield.

⚽ What is the strangest criteria to decide which clubs enter a cup?

The Inter-Cities Fairs Cup, which UEFA like to call 'the father of European football tournaments', was initially open to teams from the 60 or so cities across Europe which hosted major industrial trade fairs. Ernst Thommen, a Swiss pools magnate on FIFA's executive committee, had, as UEFA's official history puts it, 'the idea of juxtaposing commerce and football' and thought this tournament 'could constitute the ideal meeting point for sport and business'.

This strange beast kicked off on 4 June 1955, three months before the European Cup, so the honour of scoring the first goal in a UEFA competition goes to Eddie Firmani, who found the net in the 35th minute as a London XI beat a Basel XI 5-0 in Switzerland. These teams were true XIs, drawn from various clubs within the city that hosted the trade fair. Some cities didn't like this idea, though, so Birmingham City FC were the sole representatives from the Venice of the Midlands.

The idea of playing fixtures to coincide with trade fairs meant that the first competition staggered to a conclusion three years after the first match with Barcelona trouncing a London XI 8-2 on aggregate. After the second tournament, city teams became the exception rather than the norm. In 1960–61, the criteria changed, with UEFA taking a hand in the organisation, and the Fairs Cup was opened to top clubs who weren't involved in either the European Cup or the Cup Winners' Cup and was completed within a season.

The new, improved competition was used to test new rules: away goals gave Dynamo Zagreb the edge in their 1966–67 tie with Dundee United and Spartak Trnava edged past Olympique de Marseille after a penalty shoot-out in 1970. It was renamed the UEFA Cup in 1971, metamorphosing into the UEFA Europa League in 2009. But before it ceased to be the Fairs Cup, the competition spawned a mutant knockout tournament called the Anglo-Italian Cup.

In 1969, Swindon Town were the shock winners of the League Cup but, as a Third Division side, were not allowed entry into the Fairs Cup; the same fate had befallen QPR, League Cup winners in 1967. Concerned that this rule unduly punished such plucky giant killers, the Football League created the Anglo-Italian League Cup, in which the League Cup winners took on the Coppa Italia holders. This was something of a departure for the Football League which was then

run by Alan Hardaker, a man who famously said he didn't like European football because there were 'too many wops and dagoes'. Yet Swindon enjoyed their European campaign, losing 2-1 to AS Roma in the Stadio Olimpico and winning 4-0 at the County Ground, against a side that included Fabio Capello.

The Anglo-Italian League Cup inspired – and was succeeded by – the Anglo-Italian Cup. Rapidly becoming *calcio*'s nemesis, Swindon won this competition, too, in

1970, awarded victory in Naples when the game was abandoned due to crowd trouble when they were 3-0 up against Napoli. The Anglo-Italian kept going in various forms, including a semi-professional phase from 1976 to 1986, and then a brief second-tier professional revival in the 1990s.

These tournaments soon spawned a host of pre-season competitions. The Watneys Cup, contested by the top scoring side in the four divisions of the Football League, is chiefly notable because, in the 1970 semi-final between Manchester United and Hull City, Denis Law made history as the first man to miss from the spot in a penalty shoot-out. This competition – and its rival Texaco Cup – are still remembered with a rosy, nostalgic glow. The same could not be said for the Full Members Cup (1985–92), created to fill the gap left in the fixture schedules by UEFA's ban on English clubs after the Heysel tragedy.

One glance at the list of miscellaneous cup competitions between national sides on rsssf.com proves that countries will find any excuse to start a football tournament. The more obscure knockout competitions include the Eco Tournament (contested in 1993 by seven countries in a regional trade pact: Azerbaijan, Iran, Kazakhstan, Kyrgyzstan, Pakistan, Tajikistan and Turkmenistan), the Games of the New Emerging Forces (mainly contested by Communist states in Asia and Africa between 1963 and 1965, but also briefly featuring university teams from Argentina and Uruguay) and the Arab Police Championship (no explanation necessary).

As odd as these all sound, they are not quite as weird as the laudable but transient Glasgow Dental Cup. This was staged once, in 1928, to raise funds to build, as the name suggests, a new dental hospital in Scotland's biggest city. Contested by five clubs – Celtic, Clyde, Partick Thistle, Queen's Park, Third Lanark and Rangers (who mysteriously entered at the semi-final stage) – it raised £819 (£40,000 in today's money). In the final, on 11 December 1928 in front of 5,000 spectators, Partick beat Rangers 2-0 with a goal from Davie Ness and a penalty by John Torbet, who banged in 116 goals for the Jags.

● What was the earliest kick-off time for a professional game?

Fans like to bemoan the fact that, these days, there are almost as many kick-off times as there are games. And it's not just a British disease. On the weekend of 17/18 November 2012, all 10 Spanish Liga fixtures kicked off at different times. Pay-per-view television doesn't like too many simultaneous matches. What especially annoys supporters, if they come from countries with a tradition of away support, is that matches seem to start earlier and earlier. Many leagues, like Spain's, now pander to lucrative faraway markets with a considerable time difference. In Scotland, potentially troublesome games often kick off as early as noon to restrict pre-match drinking.

Mind you, it's not easy to clarify what is a traditional kick-off time. In Britain, 3pm on a Saturday is regarded as the hallowed, classic kick-off time. Queen's Park claim they were the first to adopt this as their customary kick-off time, though that's hard to establish. It is recorded, however, that on the day league football began – Saturday, 8 September 1888 – only one game started at that time: Aston Villa v Wolverhampton Wanderers. If you look at the results of that day, you'd presume that Fred Dewhurst has the honour of having scored the first-ever goal in league football, because he found the target for Preston North End against Burnley after all of three minutes. But that game kicked off at 3.50pm, which means it was seven minutes to four when Dewhurst scored. At that

If only they had fixed a regular 3pm kick-off time, Gershom Cox would have avoided infamy - as the first league (own) goalscorer.

time, Villa and Wolves were already enjoying their half-time tea with the score at 1-1. The visitors had taken the lead on the half-hour, at 3.30pm, when Villa defender Gershom Cox fumbled the ball across his goal line, scoring an own goal that entered the record books.

Kick-off times have always been more diverse than the conventional wisdom suggests. Italy's Serie A traditionally plays on Sunday afternoons, while games in Spain used to kick off late on Sunday evenings. In Germany, fans will tell you that the classic kick-off time is almost the same as in England, namely 3.30pm on a Saturday. But that's not quite true. On the Bundesliga's very first matchday – Saturday, 24 August 1963 – every game kicked off at 5pm, a common time during this inaugural season. In the decades before the Bundesliga, games in Germany were normally played on Sundays because many of the players, who were semi-pros or amateurs, worked on Saturdays.

One wonders how they would have reacted if they had been told their next league game would kick off five minutes after midnight on a Wednesday. That's when Barcelona's home game against Sevilla began on 3 September 2003.

The story behind this unusual time was a dispute between Sevilla and Barcelona's new president Joan Laporta. When Laporta realised that nine of the internationals in Barça's squad would have to play for their respective countries on the Saturday after this game, scheduled for Wednesday, he asked Sevilla to move the match to Tuesday. But Sevilla president José del Nido refused on the grounds that his team faced Atlético Madrid the Sunday before. Whereupon an angry Laporta threatened that if Sevilla insisted on Wednesday, Barcelona would choose a kick-off time as close to Tuesday as possible, namely shortly after midnight. Sevilla called his bluff – and Laporta was true to his word.

'This is a throwback to the Spain of guitars and tambourines, when every ruse was legit,' Sevilla's skipper Pablo Alfaro complained. And Javier Irureta, then coaching Deportivo La Coruña, said: 'What do you think your wife's going to say when you tell her you're going to a football game at midnight? She thinks you're cheating on her!' But when Laporta noted how much publicity he was getting and that there was nothing in the Spanish FA's statutes that prevented him from doing it, he went ahead with his plan. The game started at 0.05am, watched by 80,200 fans at the Camp Nou. It finished 1-1. Barcelona's new signing Ronaldinho equalised with a wonder goal on his home debut, capping off a solo run across half the length of the pitch. At 1.24am.

⚽ Can elephants take penalties?

They have been known to do so occasionally, albeit not in a competitive match on a conventional football pitch. One of them was so good at it that he beat a group of professional footballers in a penalty shoot-out. The pachyderm in question was a performer in 'Lord' George Sanger's travelling circus. The title was self-awarded, but it suited the eccentric millionaire's image and looked good on posters. His wife used to dance in the lions' cages but Sanger, though he loved working with any animals, was particularly fond of elephants.

According to Andrew Ward's *Football's Strangest Matches*, this particular elephant was so good that when the circus hit Leicester in the late 1890s, Sanger issued a challenge to the city's professional footballers. Four Leicester Fosse players duly accepted and took on the elephant.' Each contestant had to take four penalties and then go between the sticks and try to keep out his opponent's four shots.

LORD JOHN SANGER AND

(LIMITED).

GREAT BRITAIN'S LARGEST AND GRANDEST AMUSEMENT

THE LARGEST AND GRANDEST SHOW IN THE W

Founded in 1837 by John Sanger (the Eldest and Original Sanger). The only Travellin has been commanded by Her Majesty the Queen to appear at Windsor Ca

**THE FIRST VISIT OF LORD JOHN SANGER AND SONS', LTD., A
ENGLISH SHOW.**

**THE GREATEST NOVELTY IN THE WORLD! THE ELEPHANTS
FOOTBALL MATCH.**

FOOTBALL MATCH, ELEPHANT V. MAN,

For a very MASSIVE GOBLET, which will be on view at Mr. W. H. RUSSELL'
Mr. W. KEECH, Centre Forward, Loughborough Football Club, has arranged to compet
CENTRE FORWARD ELEPHANT, which can kick the most goals out of
Mr. W. KEECH and the ELEPHANT to keep goal in turn

To this day, Leicester fans stubbornly point out that the elephant's size gave him a bit of an edge when he went in goal. (Chelsea's man mountain of a keeper, William 'Fattie' Foulke, used the same tactic at about the same time.) The ball also happened to be six times larger than normal. Which is why FIFA's official home page says: 'Back in the 1890s, long before there were any FIFA standards governing the circumference of the ball, an elephant caused red faces among the professional players at English club Leicester Fosse when Sanger's Circus bet that no one could score past its elephant in a penalty shoot-out using an oversize ball.' This is, in fact, nonsense. There were no FIFA standards regarding the ball at the time, because FIFA didn't actually exist. The FA, however, had strict regulations governing the size of the ball.

On this particular occasion, the shoot-out was not held under FA rules, thus the famous, but sadly anonymous, elephant could take on the Leicester players, three of whom were soundly beaten and shall thus remain equally nameless. The fourth was William Keech who, says Ward, 'used a crafty penalty-taking technique. Keech feinted to take the ball one side of the elephant, then, as the elephant raised his foot in anticipation, Keech slotted the ball into the other corner.' Steve Russell, of the website Independent Rs, adds: 'He went on to repeat this trick successfully but when Keech took his turn in goal, the elephant copied the same trick and scored twice in the same fashion. This resulted in a replay and Keech once again deceived the elephant with the same tactic and won the competition by three goals to two.'

Keech was almost as well-travelled as the elephant he defeated. He was born in Irthlingborough in 1872 and while he is best known as a Liverpool, Leicester and Queen's Park Rangers player, he also played for Wellingborough, Finedon, Kettering Hawks, Irthlingborough Wanderers, Barnsley St

Peter's, Blackpool, Loughborough Town, Brentford and Kensal Rise United. According to Tony Williamson's book about the history of QPR, Keech later became 'a billiards marker' (a man who keeps scores made by players and indicates them on a scoring board). One of the pubs he regularly worked in was on 464 Harrow Road in North Kensington, London; it was, of course, called The Elephant and Castle.

⚽ Do footballers have small feet?

In Eva Menasse's novel *Vienna*, the heroine's footballing father declares: 'The best footballers have small feet.' This is certainly a popular theory – the great Bulgarian Hristo Stoitchkov once attributed his success to his size 5 feet – but is it true?

There is no shortage of famous players with dainty feet. The smallest foot size we have come across in professional football is size 2 (though other reports say 3 and 4), worn by Johnny Hancocks (pictured), the England inside-right whose blistering shot helped him score 158 goals for Wolves, with whom he won the league in 1954. And when we say blistering we mean it quite literally: his tough manager Stan Cullis once made the mistake of saving a Hancocks penalty in training and needed physio on his injured hand for a fortnight.

Brazilian striker Adhemar had size 3.5 feet. Lothar Matthäus and Romania's most naturally gifted footballer Gheorghe Hagi wore size 5 boots, while David Villa, like Roberto Carlos, wears size 6. Gerd Müller preferred size 7 and 6.5. In his 1973 autobiography, Der Bomber recalled: 'I have healthy feet but they do not have the same size. Football boots need to feel like a second skin and so adidas manufactures them specially for me – the left larger than the right.' This disproves the legend that Müller wore boots too big for him because they helped him turn more quickly.

Jackie Milburn, the Newcastle and England centre-forward, was so keen to make his boots feel like a second skin that he says in his memoirs: 'I always wore a size 6 boot even though

Jackie Milburn's boots.

my feet were size 8, so I used to break them in by wearing them without socks and soaking them in cold water until they moulded to my feet.' To ensure his boots were broken in beyond reasonable doubt, Milburn wore them down the pit when he worked as a miner.

The Toon legend's concept is not unusual. The great Austrian midfielder Johann 'Buffy' Ettmayer, who played for Eintracht Frankfurt in the 1970s, always chose a smaller size because, as he famously put it, 'football boots have to be like condoms for your feet'. Lionel Messi (popularly supposed to wear size 10 boots) likes 'boots to be really tight so they adjust to your feet and seem more like slippers than shoes'.

The experience of Argentinian midfielder Mafias Alameda, who signed for Sevilla in 1996, shows how perilous big boots can be. More than 10,000 supporters gathered at the club's Ramón Sánchez Pizjuán stadium to welcome him but the introduction soon went horribly awry. 'I realised they were mistaken about me, I was a midfield destroyer, not a striker,' Alameda recalled. 'And I'd forgotten my boots. Someone gave me a pair, but they were size 10.5 or 11, and I'm a 9.5. The crowd started chanting for tricks, but I couldn't control the ball, it ended up in the stands.'

With vicious irony, when rebellious midfielder Matthias Sammer was deemed to be getting too big for his boots by officials at Dynamo Dresden in the 1980s, they ensured that, when the whole squad received new footwear, Sammer's were three sizes too large. 'It was pure harassment, individualism wasn't tolerated,' he said.

Giacinto Facchetti had the opposite problem. When he started at Inter in the 1960s, the conventional wisdom in Serie A was that any player whose feet were bigger than size 7.5 couldn't be a good player. His Inter team-mate Sandro Mazzola recalled, 'Giacinto bandaged his toes with sticking plaster before games to squeeze his feet into a smaller boot size. Jair saw him and ribbed him, "Giacinto, you can't put Milan inside Treviglio" [a small town near Milan].'

The average shoe size in the UK is 9 – Wayne Rooney's boot size – and players typically wear size 8.5 to 9.5 boots. Famous footballing Bigfoots include Peter Crouch, whose robot dance celebration might have looked less tacky if he didn't have size 11 feet; Günter Netzer, who wreaked havoc in midfield in the 1970s with size 12 feet; and Nigerian striker Kanu who bamboozled opponents with his tricky size 15 feet.

Garrincha, the tragic Brazilian genius who won two World Cups, probably had the most enigmatic feet in football.

Stricken by polio as a child, the Little Bird's right leg turned inwards while his left leg turned outwards. Before kick-offs, he often stood with his feet splayed apart like a scarecrow. Because of his unusual shape and sorcery on the ball – in the first 34 seconds of a 1958 World Cup match against the Soviet Union he beat seven opponents with his dribbling skills – he was likened to a *curupira*, a demon in Brazilian rural folklore whose feet were believed to be back to front. Yet before the 1958 World Cup, doctors were astonished by results of the Brazilian squad's medical tests which showed, as biographer Ruy Castro noted, that 'in spite of being grotesquely off centre, Garrincha had the poise of an angel. They took plaster casts of all the players' feet, but no one's toes, arch and instep were as neatly aligned as Garrincha's.'

Garrincha – the Little Bird – on the ball at the World Cup 1962. The hapless defender is England's Ray Wilson.

⚽ Why did Independiente hold a minute's silence for Neil Armstrong?

The first man to walk on the moon left a very special souvenir up there: a pennant from Independiente de Avellenada. As soon as the crew for Apollo 11 was named, the club's press officer Hector Rodriguez proposed making Armstrong, Buzz Aldrin and Michael Collins members of Independiente. The membership cards – Armstrong was member No. 80,400 – and some memorabilia, including pennants, were sent to the astronauts. Armstrong wrote back thanking the club in May 1969, two months before his historic journey to the moon.

After Armstrong took his giant step on 20 July 1969, the Argentinian club's officials suggested he had left a pennant on the moon. Nobody took them too seriously until Armstrong visited Buenos Aires in November 1969 on the Apollo 11 crew's exhausting world tour. At an embassy reception, Armstrong assured Rodriguez he had taken the pennant to the moon, that it had brought him good luck and he had left it there. So when he died on 25 August 2012, the club held a minute's silence before their next home game, against Arsenal de Sarandi. As *FourFourTwo* magazine noted: 'Afterwards everyone in the stadium applauded as if Armstrong was a club legend. And in a unique way, he was.'

⚽ What was the oddest method to separate teams level on points?

Every league system has one obvious drawback – what happens if teams end up with the same amount of points? Today, we take it for granted that goal difference – when goals conceded are subtracted from goals scored – takes care of that. However, for a very long time, the more mathematically challenging goal average was in use (the number of goals scored divided by the number of goals conceded).

The goal average system seems absurd in retrospect, because it didn't reward going for goals (scoring 3 goals and conceding 1 for a goal average of 3.0 is better than scoring 10 and conceding 4 for a goal average of 2.5) as well as needing a calculator. But the French Ligue 1 used it until 1964, the German Bundesliga until 1969, and the Football League stuck with it until 1976.

One league briefly broke the mould. The Soviet Union had switched from goal average to goal difference as early as 1961 but felt this was not a great way of deciding titles or relegations. So there were regular play-off games from 1961 to 1977 to decide who won the league and who went down. For the rest of the table, goal difference remained the first tie-breaker … with one exception.

In 1970, the powers that be hit upon a fantastic new idea. For this one season, the new tie-breaker was the number of footballers in a squad that played for the national team. After taking such a revolutionary step – quite a bold one given the stagnation that typified the USSR under Brezhnev – the authorities scrapped this system the next year. The difficulty may have been that not many clubs had internationals in their squads. The USSR's 1970 World Cup squad, for example, contained players from seven clubs – and two of those, CSKA Moscow and Dynamo Moscow, were involved in the play-off for the title. So in a league containing 17 clubs, this rule could easily end up making absolutely no difference whatsoever. So it was back to boring old goal difference in 1971.

🄯 What formation did North Korea play in 1966?

When North Korea qualified for the World Cup in 1966, they didn't have diplomatic relations with the hosts, England. After some sporting diplomacy, the team were allowed to participate as long as their national anthem wasn't played before games. Inspired – or terrified – by their great leader Kim Il-Sung (who urged them, 'As the representatives of the Africa and Asia region, as coloured people, I urge you to win one or two matches'), they surprised everyone by knocking out Italy, and then reaching the quarter-finals, where they raced into a 3-0 lead against Eusébio's Portugal before losing 5-3. Their heroic overachievement was one of the highlights of the tournament but opinion still differs over their formation.

To Western eyes, their game was distinctly unusual. Dennis Barry, a Middlesbrough fan who watched their group games at Ayresome Park, told the BBC: 'They played good football. They were small and that was a novelty in itself. It was like watching a team of jockeys playing. They moved the ball around really well and they played attacking football. There was nothing defensive about their game.' Their manager, Myung Rye Hyun (the name means 'Sternly Rising Sun'), attributed their success to a fast, position-swapping style of play he called *Chollima Lightning Football* (Chollima was a horse that, according to Far Eastern mythology, could run at 1,000 miles an hour.) Dan Gordon, who produced a BBC documentary on the team, hailed them as pioneers. 'Football was incredibly slow in 1966. Nowadays teams play fast, like the Koreans in 1966.'

Forget Total Football. The Koreans modelled themselves on a horse that could run at 1,000 miles per hour.

Perhaps because the country's football developed in such extreme isolation, there has been talk that the North Koreans played in a formation the game had never seen before. Wilhelm Fischer, in his book *Fussball Weltmeisterschaft*, published in Germany a week after the final, suggested they played 'an unusual 9-1-1 formation' against Chile before incongruously adding that they 'either defended with eleven men or attacked with nine'.

Yet the FIFA technical report on the finals doesn't mention any such system which, given that it comments on Uruguay's 1-4-3-2, it surely would have if Korea's formation had been so revolutionary. Is it possible that, given the speed of their play, their tireless efforts, and their attacking style, such an unusual formation could have gone unnoticed by a panel of experts which included one former England manager (Walter Winterbottom) and one future Three Lions boss (Ron Greenwood)?

The best books about those finals don't clarify anything. Most don't even mention Korea's tactics, a few have them playing 4-2-4 while another says that, at times, they played three up front. Brian Glanville, in his definitive *The Story of the World Cup*, describes them as a 'team of little men who moved sweetly and finished splendidly'. It is just possible that their movement, attacking play and pace, and what Glanville refers to as 'the charisma of the unknown', convinced less informed observers that their formation was radically different.

What is an Olympic goal?

An Olympic goal is what South Americans call a goal scored direct from a corner. On 2 October 1924, Uruguay returned from winning gold at the Olympic football tournament in Amsterdam, and Argentina beat them 2-1 in a friendly with a goal scored in just such fashion.

The scorer was left-winger Cesáreo Onzari. The goal made this stalwart of Atlético Huracán famous across Argentina. In *Football In Sun And Shadow*, Eduardo Galeano notes: 'It was the first time in the history of football a goal was scored that way. The Uruguayans were speechless. When they found their tongues, they protested. They claimed their goalkeeper was pushed when the ball was in the air. Then they howled that

Onzari's 'Olympic Goal' for Argentina against Uruguay. Did the wind get an assist? It depends on your nationality.

Onzari hadn't intended to shoot at the net and that the goal had been scored by the wind.'

As you might expect, the goalscorer insisted then – and for the next 40 years of his life – that the ball had done just what he intended. 'Maybe the keeper got out on the wrong side of the bed that day,' he reflected later. 'Or players may have blocked his path. But I never scored a goal like that again. To be honest, when I saw the ball go in, I couldn't believe it.' Such a strike was so rare it became known, either – as Galeano says – 'in homage or in irony' as the 'Olympic goal'.

Onzari's timing was certainly remarkable. Scoring straight from a corner had only become legal since the beginning of August 1924, after the International Football Association

Board decided to change the rules. However, FIFA disagrees with Galeano about Onzari's being the first goal to be scored in such a fashion. The game's blazers-in-chief say that a little known Scottish striker called Billy Alston scored straight from a corner in the Scottish Second Division in late August.

Inspired by the legend of Onzari's goal, other Argentinian footballers sought to emulate him. One of the most effective was Juan Ernesto Cochoco Alvarez. In six seasons at Colombian side Deportivo Cali, he only scored 35 goals – but eight of them were direct from corners. He once scored twice from a corner in the same game. The secret, he said, was a training ground competition with Colombian teammate Angel Maria Torres to see who could score the most from corners.

Anibal Francisco Cibeyra wasn't quite as prolific. But playing for Ecuador's Emelec in the 1970s, he once scored three Olympic goals in successive derbies against Barcelona de Guayaquil, a feat that earned him the nickname *El Loco De Los Goles Olimpicos* (The Olympic Goal Fanatic).

Such fanaticism looks less extreme when you consider: Eintracht Frankfurt star Bernd Nickel who has scored an Olympic goal from all four corners of the club's ground; Morten Gamst Pedersen who as a junior player in Norway scored six from corners in the same match; and Northern Ireland international Charles Tully who, in 1953, scored directly for a corner for Celtic against Falkirk and, when the goal was disallowed because the ball wasn't in the arc, retook the corner and scored again.

Most prolific of all is the great Turkish striker Sükrü Gülesin who, between 1940 and 1954, scored 32 Olympic goals. As Özgür Canbas, a presenter on Turkey's Radio Spor, noted: 'His major characteristic was that he could score from the left and the right sides even though he was left-footed.'

⚽ Why can't you score an **own goal** from a direct free-kick?

The rules on this are clear, even though few people are aware of them. Law 13 states: 'If a direct free-kick is kicked directly into the team's own goal, a corner kick is awarded to the opposing team.' When you think about it for a second, Law 13 is a bit odd. If you're awarded a direct free-kick and decide to hit the ball in the general direction of your own goal, possibly because you want to involve your goalkeeper, the free-kick should be considered taken the moment the ball leaves your foot – and after that, officials should let events take their course.

But the custodians of the game felt it would be profoundly unfair if you could score an own goal from such a set-piece. You can't concede an own goal from an indirect free-kick because someone else has to touch the ball. So if you could score an own goal straight from a direct free-kick, your opponents would, in a circuitous way, be rewarded for the severity of their infringement.

You might think that the question was entirely academic, but Wally Downes proved otherwise. It's been 30 years since he made his mark by scoring an own goal from a free-kick.

The telling and retelling of the tale may have added the odd flourish here and there. What we know is this: on 27 December 1983, Wimbledon played Millwall at Plough Lane in the old Third Division. Going into stoppage time, the Dons led 4-2 and had just been awarded a free-kick, which was taken by midfielder Downes. He turned around, hit the ball towards his own goal and somehow it went in, past mystified keeper Dave Beasant. The referee pointed towards the centre circle to make the score 4-3. Luckily for Downes, the Dons held on for another five minutes to win the match.

Now, it's entirely possible that Downes wanted to play a back pass, missed the goalkeeper and was unlucky that referee John E. Martin, oblivious to the arcane Law 13, didn't seem to know the appropriate rule and failed to award Millwall a corner. But it could have been a prank. An inveterate practical joker, Downes is the player who some credit as starting the myth of Wimbledon's Crazy Gang. He once called a TV show Dave Beasant was on, claiming to be a Liverpool official and offering him the chance to leave the hopeless Dons. In any case, as Downes left the pitch, he told a reporter that the referee didn't know the laws of the game and the goal shouldn't have been allowed to stand. He, for one, was well-versed in Law 13.

⚽ Who is the greatest penalty saver in football history?

After saving three Valencia spot-kicks to win Bayern Munich the UEFA Champions League in 2001, Oliver Kahn said of the shoot-out, 'I reached a level of concentration I had never been before. I felt like I was on an undetected planet.'

Kahn hadn't, hitherto, stopped that many penalties but that didn't matter much in Germany where the prevailing view is that great keepers, like Kahn and Sepp Maier, don't necessarily stop spot-kicks. There are certain exceptions to this rule, notably Gianluigi Buffon and Edwin van der Sar, but even Liverpool fans might agree that their shoot-out heroes Bruce Grobbelaar and Jerzy Dudek weren't world-class.

Indeed, one of the most effective penalty stoppers in English football – Paul Cooper, who saved eight out of ten for Ipswich Town in 1979–80 – never won a cap at any level for England. And Steaua Bucharest icon Helmuth Duckadam,

Gotcha! Helmut Duckadam saves Barcelona's fourth and final penalty to win the 1986 European Cup for Steaua Bucharest.

who saved all four penalties to clinch the 1986 European Cup final, won just two caps for Romania and was fourth choice behind Silviu Lung, Dumitru Moraru and Vasile Iordache.

Duckadam's saves in Seville show why Germans don't take penalty-stopping too seriously. The first three penalties – taken by Barcelona's José Ramón Alexanko, Angel Pedraza and Pichi Alonso (Xabi's dad) – were shot at the same spot: low and to the keeper's right. If Duckadam guessed correctly he was bound to make contact with the ball. The fourth taker, Marcos, aimed at the other side, but low enough for the Steaua keeper to block easily if he went the right way. Nonetheless, saving four penalties in a row is a feat no other keeper has matched in a game of that magnitude.

🌑 Which teams won the league and were relegated next season?

It is richly symbolic of Manchester City's proud record of false dawns and flashy underachievement that they should hold this dubious distinction in England. What's more, when they slipped out of the old First Division in 1937–38, they did it the hard way, contriving to finish 21st out of 22, despite scoring 80 goals, more than any other team, and registering the season's biggest away win, trouncing Derby County 7-1 at the Baseball Ground.

No team in England has duplicated this dubious achievement. The only other major European league in which anything like this has ever happened is the German Bundesliga, where Nuremberg won the title in 1968 and were relegated a year later, fair and square, on the field of play, without any deductions of points or other penalties.

If it's any consolation for City, the relegation of reigning champions is a common phenomenon in Scandinavia. Thanks to some truly exhaustive research by Karel Stokkermans, one of the founders of the Rec.Sport.Soccer Statistics Foundation, we know it has happened four times in Sweden (the most recent victims being IFK Gothenburg in 1970) and Norway, and three times in Denmark and Finland. Stokkermans concludes that Finland is 'the only country which had reigning champions relegated in consecutive years'. Tampereen Pallo-Veikot won the Veikkausliiga in 1994, then went down in 1995 just as Haka Valkeakoski lifted the championship only to be relegated themselves in 1996.

In an answer that testifies to the predictably unpredictable nature of football, it would be remiss not to mention Algerian club EP Sétif. Champions in 1987, they were relegated in 1988 – and won the African Cup of Champion Clubs, the only team from outside the top flight to do so.

🌑 What is the strangest sending off?

One of the odder stories of English football in 2013 was when the Chelsea player Eden Hazard, showing all the class that his club had displayed throughout the season, was sent off for kicking one of Swansea City's ball boys, who was doing a spot of actorish time-wasting in a League Cup semi-final. It was put forward, with some justice, as one of the strangest sendings off of all time. But, of course, given football's rich history, there are plenty of rival claims.

Swinging on the crossbar – and breaking it twice – earned Athlone Town goalkeeper Mick O'Brien a red card in an Irish Cup semi-final against Finn Harps at Oriel Park on 31 March 1974. Before you rush to the judgement that the referee was an officious killjoy, it's worth pointing out that the first breakage had taken fifteen minutes to fix while the second forced the PA announcer to ask, 'Is there a carpenter in the ground?'

At St Mel's Park, Athlone's home ground, the crossbars were made of metal. Trusting in their resilience, O'Brien had got used to swinging on the bar to entertain fans, stave off boredom or, he said, to 'make sure the ball went over'. Oriel Park's wooden crossbars were not made for swinging. When play resumed after the first breakage, Finn Harps scored two quick goals to make it 4-0 and O'Brien was seen to climb the netting and throw himself bodily onto the bar, bringing the whole goal crashing down. That earned him a straight red card, the derision of the Irish media and a half-hearted defence from manager Amby Fogarty who declared, 'he is very dedicated and a bit headstrong'.

Some Athlone fans suggested his antics were prompted by shame at the team's abject performance but O'Brien had his own explanation for his behaviour. 'I was trying to fix it when it came crashing down on me. The corner of the post seemed a bit loose so I jumped up to mend it. When I touched it the post came away in my hand.' He then explained why somersaults and swinging on crossbars had become such an essential part of his game: 'I think I might be over-fit'.

Lest you assume O'Brien was merely trying too hard to prove the cliché that goalkeepers are crazy, it is only fair to add that, on 22 October 1975, he kept a clean sheet when Athlone held AC Milan to a 0-0 draw in the UEFA Cup.

⚽ What are the oddest reasons for stopping play?

Failing floodlights, holes suddenly appearing on the pitch during play (famously caused by subsidence at Watford's Vicarage Road ground in a match against Grimsby in December 1961) all sound pretty humdrum alongside the remarkable story of the ten-minute stoppage during a reserve match in Florence in 1954.

On 27 October 1954, in Tuscany's most famous city, Fiorentina played US Pistoiese in the now forgotten Campionato Riserve, Italy's reserve team league. The reports agree that some 10,000 people were on hand at the Stadio Comunale. That seems an astonishing crowd for a reserve game against what was then a fourth-division club. But that Wednesday afternoon Fiorentina gave their entire first team a brief run-out during the first half. Eight of these men – including the great Swedish forward Gunnar Gren – would win Serie A the following season, so maybe word had spread.

And supporters who came out to see their stars also saw something entirely unexpected.

In the second half, Fiorentina played their normal reserve team. But a few minutes after the restart, at roughly 2.30pm, the referee noticed a noise from the stands out of all proportion to what was happening on the pitch. He could see spectators pointing at the sky and when the players began looking up he finally halted play. 'I saw something like small rings in the distance,' Pistoiese's captain Romolo Tuci later said. 'What they actually were I really don't know.'

Many others, however, saw much more clearly. Reports speak of at least 20 unidentified flying objects in various shapes and sizes in what remains one of the best-documented UFO sightings in history. The objects had previously hovered

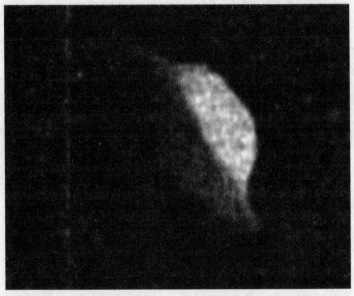

One of the alien spacecraft that came to watch Fiorentina's reserves on 27 October 1954.

over Florence's Duomo for so long that eye-witnesses had jammed newspaper phone lines and journalists were despatched to catch the second sighting of that day, over the Stadio Comunale. When the objects eventually whizzed out of sight, they dropped so much of the substance that ufologists call 'angel hair' that it looked as if snow was falling over Florence. After a break in play of ten minutes, Fiorentina and Pistoiese resumed their game. (On the same day, these objects were also sighted over Venice.)

With Italian football having such a defensive reputation at the time, it is tempting to assume that the crews in these UFOs might have been bored rigid by the dourness of the sporting spectacle below. Yet the visitors from outer space struck lucky: there was almost certainly no *catenaccio* on display in Florence on that day. Fiorentina were coached by the legendary Fulvio Bernardini, who preferred a version of the W–M system that prefigured Brazil's 4-2-4. Unusually for an Italian coach, Bernardini once declared: 'Tactics are not important. A team is only as strong as the feet of its players.' So if they do play football in space, it's probably fun to watch.

⚽ What is football's strangest transfer deal?

There is an apocryphal tradition that Aston Villa acquired a player from Gillingham in 1937 for three used turnstiles, two goalkeeper tops, three cans of weed killer and a typewriter, but it's hard to find any proof that this deal ever happened.

To stick with transfers we know definitely did happen, Roger Fallas's move from Costan Rican second division club Puma to Universidad de Costa Rica in July 2013 was for 50 footballs. The 26-year-old defender's contract was running out so, instead of a fee, Puma's technical director Rigoberto Chinchilla requested footballs. Universidad were happy to oblige.

Being sold for a bag of balls might sound a tad undignified but other members of the footballing profession have been traded for much more embarrassing commodities. In the English game, tracksuits and training kits were used to facilitate the moves of John Barnes (from Sudbury Court to Watford), Tony Cascarino (from Crockenhill to Gillingham) and Gary Pallister (from Billingham Town to Middlesbrough). Although Manchester United's club record fee is £30.7m for Dimitar Berbatov, in 1927 they snapped up half-back Hugh McLanahan after donating a freezer full of ice cream to Stockport County.

Players' frequent lament that clubs buy and sell them like meat took on a horribly literal meaning in February 2006 when Romanian club UT Arad sold defender Marius Cioara to fourth division side Regal Horia for 15kg of meat. The buying club was understandably upset when, days later, Cioara decided to give up football to find a job in Spain in agriculture or construction. A Regal Horia official complained, 'we lost twice – we lost a good player and our team's meat for a week.'

In Norway, a country which consumes around 105,000 tonnes of seafood a year, shrimp were used to facilitate the move of Kenneth Kristensen from third division club Vindbjart to local rivals Floey. The 23-year-old desperately wanted to play for Floey so Vindbjart president Vidar Ulstein proposed that he be sold for his own weight in shrimp. Kristensen was duly weighed before the next game between the clubs and the fee was agreed: 75kg in shrimp.

The oddest free transfer in the game's history must surely be the arrival of Al-Saadi Gaddafi, third son of the Libyan dictator, at Perugia in 2003. Gaddafi, an inside-forward

Al Saadi Gaddafi, son of Libyan leader Colonel Muammar Gaddafi, with Perugia president Luciano Gaucci.

who ran the Libyan FA, and fancied himself as the Libyan Maradona, was a 30-year-old billionaire when he came to Italy. The move was inspired by the player's performance for 30 minutes in a friendly in Perugia and a conversation with the club's eccentric president Luciano Gaucci that started out as a joke. Yet the player was keen and the president was curious, especially when, he insists, Silvio Berlusconi (then prime minister of Italy) told him the transfer would be politically advantageous.

The only man who didn't find any of this amusing was Perugia's coach Serse Cosmi who refused to play Gaddafi because he wasn't good enough. Given that the president boasted of sacking a youth team coach who wouldn't give Gaucci Jr a game, this was a brave stand.

The player, meanwhile, was so determined to improve and get in shape he employed Diego Maradona as his technical consultant and Canadian sprinter Ben Johnson (who won the 100m at the 1988 Olympics and was banned for taking steroids), as his personal trainer. Before Gaddafi could make his Serie A debut, he was banned when a drugs test revealed that he had too much nandrolone, the performance-enhancing steroid, in his system. Gaucci, however, managed to get the automatic two-year ban reduced to three months.

In May 2004, with Perugia leading 1-0 against Juventus in a game they needed to win to avoid relegation, Cosmi finally gave in. Signalling to his bench, he brought on Gaddafi in the 75th minute. The move had little impact: Gaddafi didn't touch the ball and Perugia held on to win. The Italian newspaper *La Repubblica* was especially scathing about the player's performance: 'Even at twice his current speed he would still be twice as slow as slow itself.'

Afterwards, Cosmi insisted that 'Gaddafi came on because he is a player and not because any of us wanted to go down in history as the one who first played the son of a head of state in the Italian championship.' Neither the change of heart – nor averting relegation – could save Cosmi, who was sacked.

His only consolation was that a year later, the club went bankrupt and Gaucci had to flee to the Dominican Republic to avoid being arrested for fraud. He has since returned to Italy. Gaucci's former protégé, Al-Saadi Gaddafi, played another ten minutes in Serie A – as a sub for Udinese the next season – before returning to Libya. During the civil war in which his father was killed, Al-Saadi fled to Niger where he has been granted political asylum by the president.

⚽ Which is the most unlikely club to break a transfer record?

Falkirk paid a world record fee of £5,000 to acquire Sydney Puddefoot in February 1922. The sale of West Ham's prolific striker almost caused a riot in east London but the club insisted the move was entirely the player's doing, saying in a statement: 'Everyone has one chance in life to improve themselves and Syd Puddefoot is doing the right thing for himself in studying his future. We understand that he will be branching out in commercial circles in Falkirk and when his football days are over he will be assured of a nice little competency.'

The truth is that Puddefoot didn't want to go. Not even when West Ham said his brother Len could move with him and he

Syd Puddefoot (right, with William Rankin) in happier times at Blackburn Rovers, where he won the FA Cup.

realised he would be paid a one-off fee of £390 (at a time when the footballer's maximum wage was £8 a week). It's possible, too, that West Ham manager Syd King didn't want to sell him. One explanation for the sale – which was oddly timed given that the Hammers were pushing for promotion – is that King named a price he thought the club would never pay. When Falkirk matched the valuation, and with West Ham in some financial difficulty, King was left with no option but to sell.

So how did Falkirk come to have the money? Their supporters raised it – indeed so generous were they that Falkirk could have paid as much as £6,000. The fans were desperate for the Bairns to regain the impetus that had led them to victory in the Scottish Cup in 1913. Scottish football was booming after the end of the First World War and with Falkirk in the top flight, the transfer might have transformed the club's prospects. It almost worked: the Bairns came fourth in 1923–24 but slid down the table when Puddefoot moved on.

Puddefoot scored 45 goals in three years at Falkirk but never really settled – he later complained that the players wouldn't pass to him – and moved on to Blackburn Rovers for £4,000. No Scottish club has ever set a world transfer record since.

Has a league-winning team ever been unable to defend their title?

The wrong answer is Juventus. The *Bianconeri* won Italy's Serie A in 2006 but, after their involvement in the Calciopoli bribe scandal was exposed, they were consigned to Serie B. But if you follow the letter of the law, Juventus were stripped of the 2006 and 2005 championships, so technically the title wasn't theirs to defend in 2006–07.

There is one very strange case of a famous, proud and strong team that couldn't defend the title they had won. This team was CSKA Moscow, the club closely associated with the Soviet army. In 1951, CSKA (then called CDSA) won the USSR's top flight by seven points and lifted the Soviet cup. But the next season, says Robert Edelmann in *A History of the People's Team in the Workers' State*, his book about Spartak Moscow, 'proved to be one of the strangest in Soviet soccer history'. The 1952 Olympics in Helsinki were to blame. For the first time, the USSR had decided to send athletes to the Games, expecting to prove the triumph of the Soviet system in the Olympian fields. 'Great attention was paid to the football competition,' says Edelmann. The 1952 season, which would have been interrupted by the Games, was cut to 13 rounds of matches, played after the Olympics, allowing the USSR team a very long time to prepare.

Boris Arkadiev, CSKA's coach, was chosen to assemble and manage the team. Roughly half the squad came from CSKA. The team beat Bulgaria in the first round, then played a legendary game against Yugoslavia, in which the Russians came back from four goals down after an hour to draw 5-5. Vsevolod Bobrov (who was also a member of the famous Russian national ice hockey team) scored a hat-trick and was on target again after six minutes of the replay. But this time the Yugoslavians came back, scoring three goals to defeat Arkadiev's men 3-1.

Edelmann writes: 'A political defeat at the hands of the representatives of the defiant Marshall Tito was intolerable.' When the sports committee concluded that CSKA Moscow were at fault for this intolerable defeat, the club's fate was sealed. The team played the first three games of the 1952 season (and won them all), but on 18 August 1952, the committee decreed that the club was to be disbanded. Thus the reigning league champions and cup winners could not defend their titles. It took the thaw that followed Josef Stalin's death in 1953 for the apparatchiks to allow CSKA to reform.

The only comparable case we know of occurred in Macau. Clube Desportivo Monte Carlo, founded in 1984, won the 2008 league title but then quarrelled with the Macau FA about a change in the regulations – whereupon the authorities swiftly banned the club for the 2009 season for 'subversiveness'.

⚽ Why did Venezia fans start booing white players?

Venezia's Ultras took a leading role in the campaign against the racist chanting that was afflicting many Italian grounds in the 1990s. As John Foot says in *Calcio: A History of Italian Football*: 'This opposition took the form of banners, leaflets and sarcasm. In one game against Verona – notorious for its hard-core support – Venezia's fans turned the racist *bu-bu* chants against Verona's white players, thereby rendering the whole concept of the chant absurd.' It wasn't exactly a long-term solution to the problem but it's hard to think of a more disconcerting riposte to racist chanting inside stadiums.

Stars

🌑 Who was Britain's first black footballer?

In 1880–81, the Scottish Football Association annual included this entry: 'Watson. Andrew: One of the very best backs we have; since joining Queen's Park has made rapid strides to the front as a player; has great speed and tackles splendidly; powerful and sure kick, well worthy of a place in any representative team.'

That entry is remarkable for what it does not say about this fine young footballer. It does not say, for example, that Watson is black – and is probably the first black footballer to play for a British club. Playing as an amateur a decade before Arthur Wharton became the first black professional footballer in Britain (keeping goal for Rotherham and Sheffield United), Watson was the first black player to win the Scottish Cup, the first black player to appear for (and captain) an international team and the first black footballer to appear in the FA Cup. Astonishingly, Watson's importance only came to light by accident in 2003 when Ged O'Brien, then a director of the Scottish Football Association's museum, spotted him in a photo of a Queen's Park line-up and realised that here was a story that could rewrite football history.

Born in 1857 in Georgetown, British Guyana, the son of a Scottish planter and a Guyanan woman, Watson came to study at King's College in London where he soon revealed a talent for football. He started playing for Queen's Park while studying natural philosophy, maths, civil engineering and mechanics. He later became club secretary, making him the first black football administrator in Britain, and won two Scottish Cups and three caps for Scotland, being appointed captain in 1881. His record was impressive: he was captain and right-back when Scotland beat England 6-1 on his debut on 12 March 1881. In his next two games, the Scots beat Wales and England 5-1.

Like many players of his era, Watson would travel anywhere to get a game, and when he moved south of the border – appearing in an FA Cup tie in 1884 for London Swifts – he effectively ended his international career, as the Scottish FA would not select footballers playing outside Scotland.

While we still don't have a full, rounded picture of Watson's career, his success is remarkable. Football was almost exclusively a white man's sport and in Glasgow, where he made his name as a footballer, Afro-Caribbeans were almost invisible in the 1870s and 1880s. The extant contemporary records do not suggest that he suffered racial abuse, one newspaper account suggesting that spectators were intrigued

Andrew Watson with members of his Scotland team that beat England at the original Hampden Park on 11 March 1882.

by the colour of his boots (brown rather than black, as was customary at the time) but not by the colour of his skin.

So Watson may have been luckier than forward Walter Tull who, while playing for Northampton Town in 1909, was abused by Bristol City fans in a manner the Northampton Echo found 'cowardly'. The nature of the abuse is clear when the correspondent tells the Bristol hooligans that 'Tull is so clean in mind and method as to be a model for all white men who play football'.

The same could be said of Watson. In 1926, the sportswriter J.A.H Catton, editor of *Athletic News*, named Watson in his all-time Scotland team. Yet long before then

Watson had drifted into the kind of obscurity typical of many footballers. After leaving Queen's Park, he had played for Bootle, Glasgow's Crusaders, and the Corinthians. After he hung up his brown boots, the consensus is that he emigrated to Australia, probably with his wife, son and daughter, where he died in around 1902, when he would have been about forty-five.

In May 2004, one hundred and two years after Watson's death, Nigel Quashie took to the field against Estonia to become the second black player to represent Scotland.

⚽ Who was the greatest diver of all time?

As with most rankings, this depends on your criteria. What do you value most – artistic expression, technical merit or originality? If it's the first, then the trophy probably has to go to German midfield genius Andreas Möller, who once went down so spectacularly that he was suspended, making him the first – and so far only – Bundesliga player to be punished for a dive after the fact, with the use of video technology.

Then again, nobody really needed technology to expose the trickery. When Möller went down on 13 April 1995, with 15 minutes to go in a match between his team Borussia Dortmund and visiting Karlsruhe, everyone on the pitch and in the stands knew the midfielder had dived. Karlsruhe's Dirk Schuster didn't just fail to make contact with Möller, he didn't get anywhere near him. When Schuster said 'a small car would have fitted between me and him', he was not greatly exaggerating. The only person who was fooled was referee Günther Habermann. He awarded Dortmund a penalty from which the home side equalised before going on to win. The

Andreas Möller in his pomp at Dortmund, secure in the knowledge that his diving is unrivalled in Europe.

dive was so blatant that the German FA suspended Möller for two games and fined him 5,000 Deutschmarks. Yet the result stood. Two months later, Dortmund were crowned league champions, one point ahead of Werder Bremen.

If you admire technical difficulty more than athleticism, it's hard not to give first prize to someone who smuggled a razor blade on to the pitch to inflict bleeding wounds upon himself. Then again, the Chilean Roberto Antonio Rojas, known to his admirers as the Condor, had an occupational advantage – as a goalkeeper he could conceal the instruments of deception in his gloves.

On 3 September 1989, Rojas kept goal for his country in a World Cup qualifier against Brazil in Rio, in front of 160,000 Brazilian fans. The first tie, also a tumultuous affair, had ended 1-1, so it all came down to this game. Brazil needed only a draw to qualify and took a 1-0 lead. Chile's hopes were ebbing away until, twenty minutes from time, Rosenery Mello do Nascimento Barcelos da Silva – a good-looking 24-year-old Brazilian girl – hurled a flare on to the pitch. It landed only a few steps away from Rojas, who went down, writhing on the ground and covering his face with his hands. By the time the physios got to him, he was bleeding profusely from facial wounds. Since no stretcher was forthcoming, his team-mates carried Rojas off the field and into the dressing room, where they stayed, refusing to finish the match.

Brazil were lucky that photographer Ricardo Alfieri Junior had taken a picture of the moment the firework hit the ground. The photo showed that the flare clearly didn't touch Rojas. FIFA then discovered he had cut himself with the blade hidden in his glove. The Chilean keeper was banned from football for life. Mello milked her notoriety. She was subsequently paid $20,000 to appear in Brazilian *Playboy*, became a model and acquired the nickname *La Fogueteira* (the pyrotechnician).

Neither Möller nor Rojas, however, can match the great Dane, Allan Simonsen, who faked his own death. In a crucial World Cup qualifier, Simonsen pretended he had been shot in the back. In 1977, director Tom Hedegaard was filming *Skytten* (*The Marksman*). The title character was a militant activist who wanted to alert Denmark to the dangers of nuclear power by killing people. His most prominent

victim was to be Simonsen. Hedegaard couldn't afford to re-enact an entire international, so the player agreed to fake his death in a real match. The shoot was on 1 May 1977, when Denmark met Poland in a World Cup qualifier in Copenhagen. When the hosts won a corner, Simonsen decided to get it all over with. As the cross came in, he started for the ball – and threw himself to the ground as if he'd been shot in the back.

It all looked halfway believable in the movie (you can see it on YouTube: search for 'Allan Simonsen vs Jens Okking'). But there was one problem. When Simonsen made his dash into the box, he lost his marker who was too slow in reacting.

Allan Simonsen about to fake his own death, live, in front of a capacity crowd for a World Cup qualifier. You couldn't make it up.

As the cross sailed in, the striker would have been in a good position to make contact with the ball ... if he hadn't dived. So there were losers all around: *Skytten* flopped, Simonsen didn't get an Academy Award and Denmark lost the game 2-1, failing to qualify for the World Cup in Argentina.

🌐 How two-footed are two-footed players?

Not very two-footed. Intrigued some years ago by an injury to Graeme Le Saux, and the ensuing media panic about England's dearth of left-footed players, Bangor University's Dr David Carey began researching footedness in football. He found that four out of five players were right-footed and, after studying nine games at the 1998 World Cup, plotting every touch, found that every player had a strong preference for one foot. Although the media is full of praise for certain two-footed players, Carey's research suggested that the genuinely two-footed player, who used their feet interchangeably on a 50/50 basis, did not exist.

The closest he came to finding such a paragon player was Slovakian international Lubomir Moravcik, who used his right foot only 64 percent of the time. 'That's about as two-footed as it gets,' Carey told *Champions* magazine in 2011. Moravcik took penalties with his right foot but used his weaker left foot for other set-pieces.

German defender Andreas Brehme was another exception to the rule. 'When I was young my father would throw the ball at me alternately from the right and left,' he recalled. 'That's why my so-called weaker left foot is as strong as the right. My left foot shots are more powerful, the ones with the right are better placed, like all penalties.' He scored the winner in the

1990 World Cup final from the penalty spot – with his right foot. 'It's like choosing a weapon,' said Brehme.

Further research by English Premier League Index blogger S. McCarthy, crunching Opta stats for the English Premier League from 2008–09 to 2011–12, qualifies Carey's conclusions but doesn't seriously contradict them. He noted that Peter Odemwingie had taken 81 shots with his right foot and 85 with his left. Obviously counting shots isn't the same as monitoring touches but this does suggest that the Nigerian international is closer to the 50/50 ideal than Moravcik. Yet in many ways McCarthy's results reinforce Carey's point, with only seven players taking shots with their weaker foot more than 40 percent of the time.

Carey's studies don't suggest that bilateralism is that common in any football culture. But developing more two-footed players has long been a focus in the English game. An FA players' development adviser once told *When Saturday Comes*: 'In places like Brazil, Holland and Africa, there's an emphasis on players making decisions for themselves during games. If coaching is too regimented then, under pressure, players will revert to type and won't risk their weaker foot.'

A player's starting position is vital. If youngsters get used to taking their first step with their left, they are more likely to kick with their right. So changing that – and teaching children to kick with both feet – is one long-term answer. Yet given that a 2010 study, by Alex Bryson of the National Institute of Economic and Social Research, found that teams with more two-footed players do not amass 'significantly' more points over a season, some clubs may wonder if there is any point. Maybe the last word should go to that left-footed genius Puskás: 'In football, you have to swing with one leg and stand on the other, so I chose to stand on my right.'

⚽ Who was the first foreign footballer in the English game?

Raymond Braine could have been British football's first foreign superstar. A gifted striker, he scored over 360 goals in a 17-year-career for club and country. Belgian football was still an amateur sport in the 1920s and Braine, like many of his peers, made ends meet by running a café. When the authorities decreed that such a sideline was only permitted for reserve team players, the 23-year-old striker decided to play abroad. Clapton Orient were keen to sign him but Braine couldn't get a work permit and joined Sparta Prague instead. Burnley chairman Charles Sutcliffe, the most powerful figure in the Football League in the 1920s, had publicly declared that the 'idea of bringing in foreigners to play in league football is repulsive to the clubs, offensive to the players and a terrible confession of weakness in the management of a club.'

The target of Sutcliffe's xenophobic fury was Herbert Chapman, the Arsenal coach who had tried to sign Austrian goalkeeper Rudolf 'Rudi' Hiden and, after the player was denied a work permit, managed to recruit Dutch goalie Gerrit Keizer by insisting he was an amateur. Fearing that Braine, Hiden and Keizer would prove the first of many, the FA insisted that foreigners could only play after living in the UK for two years. This de facto ban endured until 1978.

If maverick Egyptian striker Hassan Hegazi had shown less loyalty, the FA might have felt obliged to act earlier. In 1911, this spoilt son of an Egyptian aristocrat came to London to study engineering. He had loved football ever since he had played against British soldiers as a boy, so he joined local non-league side Dulwich Hamlet. Lively, agile, with superb ball control, an eye for a pass and a taste for over-elaborate play,

Born in Accra, Arthur Wharton kept goal for Preston North End's 'Invincibles' of the 1880s before turning professional with Rotherham, Sheffield United, Stalybridge Rovers and Stockport County.

Hegazi was dubbed 'Nebuchadnezzar' by the fans. Fulham tried to buy him and he played once for the Cottagers, scoring in a 3-1 win over Leeds, but he decided, loyally, to stay with Dulwich. In 1914, he returned to Egypt, where he represented his country in two Olympic tournaments and had a street named after him in Cairo's Garden City area.

Before Hegazi, long before German striker Max Seeburg had played in the Football League for Spurs in 1908–09, and even before Ghanaian-born sportsman Arthur Wharton had become the first black footballer in the Football League in 1893–94, a Canadian full-back, Walter Wells Bowman, had

scored on his debut for Accrington on 23 January 1892 in a
4-2 victory over West Bromwich Albion.

Bowman had first come to England four years earlier, on
tour with the Canadian national team. The touring party
certainly aroused curiosity, with one paper saying: 'Some
queer ideas have been dispelled as to the colour, language and
manners of the inhabitants of Canada as shown by its representatives on the football team. The idea that foreigners can
produce something in the way of football worth going to see
is growing gradually on the mind.' A second tour, in 1891,
aimed to showcase the players in the hope that British clubs
would buy them.

Born in 1870, Bowman made his name at Berlin Rangers
in Ontario, the Canadian province where football was most
popular. On the 1891 tour, he impressed Accrington, one
of the Football League's
founder members. He
played five games for Stanley
before joining Division
Two side Ardwick and,
when that club went bust,
staying on to play for its
successor Manchester City.
Making 47 appearances
between 1892 and 1900
for Ardwick and City,
Bowman never really hit the
headlines, though he once
turned out as an emergency
goalkeeper in a derby game
against Newton Heath
(later Manchester United).
Even the indefatigable Nick

Man City's first foreign signing,
Walter Wells Bowman.

Harris, author of *England, Their England: The Definitive Story Of Foreign Footballers In The English Game since 1888*, concludes: 'What happened next remains something of a mystery.' Bowman was, Harris's researches suggest, 'last heard of in Butte, a copper mining city in Montana'.

In 2011–12, 68 nationalities were represented in the Premier League and 67 in the Championship. Canada supplied just two Premier League players – Junior Hoilett (then at Blackburn Rovers, now at QPR) and Simeon Jackson (Norwich City). In what may be a sign of how complex football nationality has become in the 120-something years since Bowman made his debut, Jackson was born in Jamaica and Hoilett, who could represent Canada or Jamaica, has hinted that he would prefer to play for England.

⚽ Who was football's first global superstar?

It has to be José Andrade – carnival musician, sometime shoe-shiner and right-half in the Uruguayan national side that won the 1924 and 1928 Olympics and the 1930 World Cup. Known as the Black Marvel or Pearl – decades before such sobriquets would be awarded to Pelé or Eusébio – Andrade once famously thrilled spectators by travelling half the pitch with the ball on his head. In his appreciation of the Uruguayan star, Eduardo Galeano says: 'The first international football icon was black, South American and poor.'

In the 1920s, Uruguay weren't just successful, they were revolutionary, playing a creative, intricate, short-passing game that Europe had never seen before, a kind of chess with a football, only possible because they shared a level of technique none of their Olympic rivals could match. Their first opponents, Yugoslavia, spied on them. Forewarned, the Uruguayans trained like clowns – and proceeded to win the match 7-0, even though their flag was raised upside down and the Brazilian anthem was played by mistake before kick-off. Uruguay's 1924 Olympics campaign was almost a ceremonial progression. Their record was: Played 5, Won 5, For 20, Against 2. They beat hosts France 5-1 in the quarter-finals before defeating Switzerland 3-0 in the final. After winning gold, they did a lap of honour, believed to be the first in the history of the event, a ritual that is still known in Spanish as 'vuelta olimpica'.

Good enough to play as full-back, down the wings or in central midfield, with enough tricks to dribble past an opponent if he couldn't pass around them, Andrade masterminded Uruguay's attacks. Asked by the media to explain the team's revolutionary style, he swore that the players trained by chasing chickens that fled, making S-shapes on the ground. The media were so credulous – and fascinated by Andrade – they published this as the truth. French football writer Gabriel Hanot, one of the inventors of the European Cup, was not fooled, writing: 'The principal quality of the victors was a marvellous virtuosity in receiving the ball, controlling it and using it. They created a beautiful football, elegant but varied, rapid, powerful, effective.' He concluded that 'these fine athletes are to the English professionals like Arab thoroughbreds next to farm horses'.

The only black player among these thoroughbreds was Andrade. The charismatic star stayed on in Paris for a while, basking in France's adoration, living as, in Galeano's words, 'a wandering Bohemian and king of the cabaret'. But he returned to South America as Uruguay faced their rivals Argentina in a hastily arranged friendly. After a 1-1 draw in Montevideo, the rematch in Buenos Aires was marred by crowd trouble. In

The Pearl – José Leandro Andrade – gets poured a half-time cup of tea at the 1928 Olympics.

the closing minutes, the home fans started throwing stones at Andrade who flung them straight back, sparking a near riot in which the Uruguayan team walked off the pitch.

Andrade – and Uruguay – would have their revenge in 1928, beating Argentina 2-1 to win their second successive Olympic gold. The organisers of the Amsterdam Games had 250,000 requests for tickets from across Europe to watch that final. Such demand led to the agreement, at the 1928 Olympics, to launch the World Cup. Andrade would be one of the best players in that first mundial even though he was already suffering from syphilis and an eye injury sustained after he crashed into a post in the 1928 semi-final.

Richard Hofmann, the German centre-forward who scored 24 goals in 25 games for the national team, said: 'Uruguay then were the best team in the world. Their star was Andrade. He was a football artist who could do simply anything with the ball and was always ahead with his thoughts by several moves.' Like so many football superstars to come, Andrade was better at reading the game than he was at reading life. He spent his last days, alcoholic, blind in one eye, in a dilapidated flat in Montevideo, with a beautiful wife, and his medals in a shoebox. He died of tuberculosis on 4 October 1957, at the age of 56. Yet for much of the 1920s, José Leandro Andrade had been the most famous footballer in the world, the player with the golden feet.

⚽ Who has scored most goals in the history of the game?

The official answer is Pelé. FIFA states unequivocally that the Brazilian legend's 1,281 goals is a world record. However, the International Federation of Football Historians and Statisticians gave their Golden Ball as the greatest goalscorer of the last century to Austrian goal machine Josef Bican, as he had been top scorer in a domestic league for 12 seasons (one more than Pelé).

Bican, the fearsome striker at the heart of Austria's Wunderteam in the 1930s, is officially credited with 649 goals by the IFFHS, although on rsssf.com his tally is enigmatically stated as '805+'. Supplementary information suggests that Bican scored another 663 in friendlies, which would give him a tally of 1,468 – 187 more than Brazil's greatest No 10. The difficulty

Artur Friedenreich (centre) with Pelé and the Brazilian football writer, Silvio de Oliveira.

here is ascertaining which friendlies and unofficial matches FIFA chooses to recognise and why. The Federation is unlikely to shift from its official position but given that the Brazilian and the Austrian scored hundreds of goals in non-competitive matches, it is hard to come to a definitive reckoning.

To confuse matters still further, another Brazilian striker has a claim to the title – the great, but largely forgotten Arthur Friedenreich. Once described as a better all-rounder than Pelé and more elegant than Alfredo di Stéfano, Friedenreich made his name in the 1910s and 1920s, scoring the goal that won Copa America for the *Selecão*. A mulatto who played in an era in Brazilian football when the game was dominated by the country's white elite, Friedenreich only managed to play by pretending, as the magazine *Placar* put it, 'to be a white man with an all-year tan'. He invented, as Eduardo Galeano wrote it in *Football in Sun and Shadow*, 'a style open to fantasy, one which prefers pleasure to results'. You could argue that he defined what we now think of the Brazilian style decades before Pelé, Didi and Garrincha. And he scored 1,329 goals – 48 more than Brazil's most famous footballer.

Unfortunately for Friedenreich, the statistical records which his father Oscar and, later, Arthur's Paulistano team-mate Mário de Andrade, lovingly compiled, which could have proved his goal tally, vanished after Andrade's death in the mid-1960s. The bereaved family are believed to have junked the records and, by the time a Brazilian football journalist tried to find them, they had disappeared into a Sao Paulo rubbish skip. In an attempt to solve the mystery, Friedenreich was tracked down to his house in Sao Paulo. As soon as the unofficial delegation of journalists and statisticians found him, they realised their quest was hopeless. He answered all their questions vaguely, while staring at an indefinite point in the distance. By the time Friedenreich died at the age of 76, on 6 February 1969, he had forgotten his name. Since his death, football has largely forgotten his claim to be the game's greatest goalscorer.

🌑 Has any footballer ever succeeded in gridiron?

It is fashionable to describe a certain style of passing midfielder – think Andrea Pirlo or David Beckham – as a quarter-back. But has any footballer ever succeeded in gridiron?

The most conspicuous success is Toni Fritsch – or Wembley-Toni as he is known to Austrian football fans of a certain age. In 1965, the speedy, diminutive winger escaped the shackles of Nobby Stiles to score twice as Austria came back from 2-1 down to win 3-2 against an England team that would win the World Cup nine months later. One of those goals, a long-range screamer with Fritsch's famous right foot, hinted at a career change to come. Six years later, when the Dallas Cowboys visited Vienna on a European tour, they were looking for a specialist place kicker. Austria coach Leopold Stastny suggested Rapid Vienna star Fritsch who had lost much of his pace but still knew how to kick a ball.

Fritsch could speak no English and had never seen an American football before. Taken to the 19th district, where some gridiron goals erected by GIs in the 1950s still stood, he booted the ball over the bar and signed a contract there and then. Delighted but bemused that he was offered money to

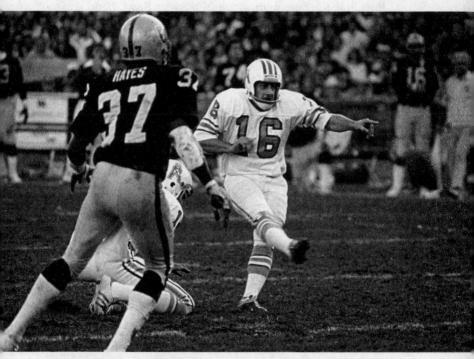

Wembley-Toni (No. 16) kicking for Houston Oilers against Oakland Raiders, towards the end of his gridiron career in the 1980s.

'play this strange sport', Fritsch quickly made an impact in Dallas. In the Cowboys first game of the 1971 season, with the scores tied against the St Louis Cardinals, Fritsch was brought on to kick a field goal. One of his opponents shouted 'Choke Fritsch choke!', but the Austrian, knowing no English, kicked the field goal and won the game. In 1972, he became the first – and, to date only – Austrian to win the Super Bowl and when he stopped kicking in 1985 he had scored 157 field goals, including 13 in consecutive play-off games. Gil Brandt, then the Cowboys personnel director, said: 'He was one of the guys from the day he got there. He knew nothing about American football, he just knew how to kick the ball.'

Fritsch is the only man to win the Super Bowl – and score twice against England at Wembley. As successful as he was in America, he never forgot the game that made him famous. When he died in 2005, of a heart attack at the age of 60, he had just collected his tickets to watch Rapid Vienna's return to the UEFA Champions League, after a nine-year absence, to face Bayern Munich.

Another Austrian Toni came close to matching Fritsch's success: Anton 'Toni' Linhart. Linhart won six caps for Austria in the 1960s and later played for the Baltimore Colts in the NFL. In 1975 and 1976, the Colts made the play-offs but didn't reach the Super Bowl, though Linhart was voted onto the Pro Bowl (the All-Star game) team in both years. In Britain, Linhart is remembered neither for his footballing skills nor for his gridiron heroics – but for playing an important part in one of the most infamous games on British soil.

On 8 May 1963, Scotland met Austria in front of 94,596 at Hampden. It was a friendly, although Scotland's Dave Mackay begs to differ. He remembers the game as inexplicably vicious, saying: 'It all started with them spitting at us. They were off their heads.' With eleven minutes left on the clock, and Scotland leading 4-1, Austria were down to eight men, because one player had been carried off injured while two others had been dismissed (Horst Nemec for dissent, Erich Hof for what the press referred to as a 'diabolical tackle at waist-height'). Mackay says the Scots weren't protecting their lead – but their leader: 'We were trying to protect Denis Law, who they were chasing like a rabbit,' he says. The one who finally got him was Austria's lone goalscorer, future NFL hero Linhart. On 79 minutes, he sent Law to the floor and when the United star didn't get up again, the disgusted referee Jim Finney had had enough. He ended the game there and then. 'I felt that I had to abandon the match or somebody would have been seriously hurt', Finney explained.

Who scored the most headers in a match?

The unlikely candidate for this honour is probably a tall, strong Brazilian striker by the name of João Ramos do Nascimento, aka Dondinho. He played for several clubs in the 1930 and 1940s, notably Atlético Mineiro and Fluminense. Why 'unlikely'? Well, as his son later wrote: 'Usually this sort of player would be English, but at that time Brazil had a footballer who scored some amazing headers called Baltazar. Everyone said that my dad was the "up-country Baltazar".'

Dondinho would probably be forgotten today if the son who wrote those words hadn't been Edson Arantes do Nascimento, better known as Pelé. In his autobiography, he added: 'It was said that Dondinho once headed five goals in the same match. Later in my career, when I reached a thousand goals, some journalists started to research this claim to see if it was true or not. And it was – they reported that the

Dinner with the Nascimentos. Dondinho is on the left, next to the teenage Pelé, who is being served up a good portion by his mum, Dona Celeste.

only goal-scoring record that didn't belong to Pelé belonged to his father!'

The matter isn't quite that clear-cut. There is some controversy about the match in which Dondinho set his record. Victor Cunha, a former president of the Atlético Três Corações, says it was a game between Atlético TC and Rio Vermelho, which the hosts won 6-1. But most sources, including old newspapers and the official home page of Pelé's former club Santos FC, point towards a match between Yuracán AC and Smart Club, two sides from the city of Itajubá, on 5 August 1939. Playing for Yuracán, Dondinho scored five headers in his team's 6-3 win. Among those witnessing this feat was Dondinho's team-mate General Eloy Menezes, later a famous equestrian who participated in three Olympic Games and became president of Brazil's National Sports Council.

⚽ Who had the **hardest shot in football?**

Before we try to answer that, let's see how hard a really hard shot really is by considering the game usually called the world's fastest team sport, ice hockey. That's because when we call a shot 'hard', what we really mean is that it travels through the air very 'fast'.

The Russian defender Alex Riazantsev is usually credited with having hit the hardest shot in ice hockey, a 114.15 mph (183.7 km/h) rocket during a skills competition in 2012. Yet, amazingly, these small, compact, hard disks – which strong men fire into the air with the help of a wooden stick that acts as a catapult – travel slower than a much larger, relatively lightweight football struck well by a human leg. Because no matter where the football record stands, you have to have a shot faster than 125 mph (202 km/h) to get anywhere close.

In February 2007, *The Guardian* published a list of hard hitters headed by Sheffield Wednesday striker David Hirst, who'd had a shot clocked at 114 mph (183.47 km/h) in 1996. Other sources pointed to a famous 125 mph (202 km/h) strike by Roberto Carlos, delivered in early 2000. Then a week later, a *Guardian* reader found a video of a goal by Brazilian hotshot Ronny Heberson Furtado de Araújo for

David Hirst, of then top-division Sheffield Wednesday, prepares to unleash his 114 mph shot.

Sporting Lisbon against Naval in November 2006. The editors calculated that Ronny's shot travelled at 131.82 mph (210.9 km/h).

We'll never know for sure who had the hardest shot, if only because conditions are never the same. The playing materials, for instance, keep changing. There are claims that Luigi Riva would have had a shot clocked at around 124 mph if he had been using a modern ball. (Riva was renowned for the power of his shots – in October 1970, one of his strikes broke the arm of a boy watching a Cagliari practice match.) Many other heroes of the past never had their shots measured. In the 1960s, the Eintracht Frankfurt player Bernd Nickel earned the nickname Dr Hammer for his ferocious shots. Nickel spent much of his childhood shooting a ball against a huge barn door. 'It's no longer there,' he says. 'Guess I've worn it out.' But his strikes were never properly timed. The same goes for Puskás. Anyone who saw him play swears that no living soul ever shot harder. Which is why he was known in Spain as *Canoncito Pum* (Booming Cannon).

Finally, sometimes a shot is too hard to be clocked. In November 2004, Anderlecht's Walter Baseggio volleyed home from the edge of the penalty area against La Louviere in the Belgian league. Baseggio hit the ball so hard that it exploded upon impact and crossed the line with the bladder hanging out. The referee allowed the goal and Anderlecht won 2-1.

🌑 Why didn't hat-trick Hurst get the 1966 World Cup final matchball?

When the final whistle rang at Wembley in 1966, West German striker Helmut Haller, who had scored the opening goal in that final, grabbed the ball and walked to the dressing room. Normally, it is the referee's duty to collect the ball but Gottfried Dienst didn't do so. Haller later explained his actions saying, 'It is an old German tradition – if the winners get the cup, the losers get the ball.'

Contrary to popular opinion in Britain, there was nothing clandestine about the way Haller made off with the ball. The unwritten rule that a player who scores a hat-trick gets to keep the match ball was then unknown in Germany. Indeed, according to the German definition, Hurst's three goals weren't even a hat-trick. To score a proper hat-trick in German football, a player had to score three goals consecutively and in the same half. Hurst later admitted that 'amid the euphoria of the World Cup win' he didn't try too hard to retrieve the ball. He certainly had the opportunity as Haller later asked all the England players and a few other stars of the tournament, such as Eusébio and Pelé, to autograph it before he took it home.

In the build-up to Euro 96, the British tabloids suddenly decided the matchball should return to England and launched an investigation into its whereabouts. This was a tad unnecessary, as Hurst had known for years that Haller had the ball.

Eventually, the Mirror Group, with support from Virgin and Eurostar UK, paid the German international (who died in 2012, at the age of 73) £80,000 for the famous pig's bladder and proudly displayed the ball at Waterloo Station.

Unfortunately, the new owners of the most famous matchball in the history of the game neglected it. 'It was left in direct sunlight and all the signatures faded,' said Mark Bushell, the marketing director of the National Football Museum, which now has the ball. 'It's unbelievable.'

⚽ Is there any real advantage in having a low centre of gravity?

In February 2011, Partizan Belgrade signed Ghanaian striker Dominic Adiyiah on loan from AC Milan. It was his header that Luis Suarez punched away in the quarter-finals of the 2010 World Cup. Milovan Rajevac, the Serbian coach of that Ghana side, said Partizan's new arrival was 'a very dangerous player, with a very low centre of gravity, explosive and quick.' When a journalist replied, 'Sounds like you are describing a player like Romário,' Rajevac said, 'Let's say they have certain similarities.' That was enough for Adiyiah, who is now playing for Arsenal Kiev, to be hailed in headlines as the 'African Romário'.

The idea that certain footballers have a low centre of gravity – and that this is an asset – has not pervaded every football culture. In Germany, pundits rarely use the phrase and, if they do, they invariably use the English words because there is no German equivalent. Elsewhere the term is used and translated almost word for word – *un centre de gravité bas* (in French) and *baricentro basso* (literally 'gravity low' in Italy. In the Spanish and South American game, where such diminutive geniuses as Maradona have shone, having a low centre of gravity is regarded as essential for a *fantastista*, the playmakers who change games with their creativity.

Although Maradona's low centre of gravity has been retrospectively lauded, it was Romário's success that made people take note of the term. The 5ft 6in forward, the greatest player in Brazil's 1994 World Cup winning side, was hailed for his stature and balance in Jimmy Burns' book on Barcelona, *A People's Passion*. As a young player, he was known as *O Baixinho*

One for the physicists to calculate as Romário sweeps past Italy's Dion Baggio in the 1994 World Cup Final. Brazil won on penalties.

(Shorty), but with the innate self-confidence that would later inspire him to paint unflattering caricatures of his enemies on the walls of his nightclub, he just ignored the nickname and focused on goals – indeed he claims to have scored over 1,000 of them. (FIFA don't agree.) Ever since he dazzled the world with his speed, power and eye for the net, many up and coming forwards have been likened to him – not just Adiyiah, but Lionel Messi, Sergio Agüero, Luis Suárez and Islam Feruz, the 18-year-old 5ft 4in striker who joined Chelsea in 2011 and is being hailed as the future of the Scotland team.

The proof that having a low centre of gravity makes for better control of the ball is convincing, if not conclusive. American youth coach Alex Kos has long argued that size does matter – the excuse clubs use when turning away prospects like Kevin Keegan because they are deemed too short – but not in the way many scouts think. A low centre of gravity, he suggests, makes it much easier for players to 'dribble, make fakes and feints, and change direction'. He also believes that coaches should 'never underestimate the toughness of a short player. They are usually tougher and more physical than taller players.' He cites Pelé (5ft 8in), Maradona (5ft 5in) and Messi (5ft 7in) in support of his case.

However, a roll call of the shortest players in the major European leagues suggests that around 5ft 3in is the threshold for players competing at this level. In other words, centres of gravity can be too low. (The shortest England internationals – Fanny Walden and Jack Crawford – played between the 1910s and 1930s and were just over 5ft 2in.)

Sometimes, having too many players built like Romário can be too much of a good thing. In Argentina, which has produced these players in industrial quantities – apart from those already mentioned, think of Pablo Aimar, Javier Saviola and Carlos Tevez – they are called *bajitos*, short ones. The

Can you win a World Cup with *bajitos*? We may soon find out. Messi, Sergio Agüero and Carlos Tevez celebrate with Maxi Rodríguez.

term is intended as a compliment so fans might say 'the coach won the game because of *los bajitos*'. Yet if they're not performing, these players can be derided *enanos* (dwarves), with their lack of stature being blamed for their failure to undo a physically imposing defence.

In recent years, Argentinian fans have demanded that Agüero, Aimar, Messi, Saviola and Tevez play in the same national side. Julio Grondona, the plain-speaking president of the Argentinian FA, dismissed the very notion saying, 'If someone wants that, better rent *Snow White And The Seven Dwarves*. You cannot use that formula to win a World Cup.' He pointed out that this kind of player might not be as useful in defence where, in his opinion, World Cups are really won. Grondona has a point: how many centre-backs get praised for their low centre of gravity?

⚽ Which player has represented the most national teams?

If we ignore the legion of players who have represented a second country – or even a third – after the first has disintegrated, two players stand out. Both of them were banned by FIFA, neither played in a World Cup finals yet they ended up playing in the same national side.

The great Alfredo di Stéfano first tasted international football with Argentina, scoring six goals in six games in the 1947 Copa America and, between 1957 and 1961, found the net an impressive 23 times in 31 appearances for Spain. While he was at Millonarios in Bogotá, he made four appearances for Colombia but those caps aren't recognised by FIFA because it had blacklisted the league (in 1948) and the national team (between 1951 and 1954) after Argentinian complaints that Colombian clubs were pirating their players (see 'What was the most entertaining league season ever?'). So, officially, if not in reality, Di Stéfano only played for two countries. He may also be the greatest footballer never to play in a World Cup finals. Argentina didn't enter in 1950 out of pique, FIFA wouldn't let him represent Spain in 1954 – and La Roja missed out on qualification anyway – and, after he had acquired Spanish citizenship, he was injured for the 1962 finals.

Millonarios (and Real Madrid) legend, Alfredo di Stéfano.

Di Stéfano may be indelibly associated with Real Madrid but he could easily have stayed at FC Barcelona had Franco not helped force through the move for the political and sporting glory of the capital and Spain over the troublesome Catalans. If Di Stéfano had stayed at Barcelona, there would have been the intriguing propsect of him sharing the limelight with the Hungarian star Ladislao Kubala, who, to quote Brian Glanville, was 'a superb player and a remarkable, somewhat Rabelaisian personality'.

The variety of countries Kubala played for offers a snapshot of his life and the tragic fashion in which wars and revolutions rewrote the history of European football in the twentieth century. Born in Budapest, to Slovak parents,

Kubala started out at Ferencvaros but was impressing up front for Slovan Bratislava when he made his debut for Czechoslovakia in October 1946. He won his sixth – and last – cap for that country in December 1947. Five months later, after returning to Budapest to avoid Czech military service, he made his debut for Hungary in a 0-0 draw away to Albania in the Balkan Cup. He was to make just two more appearances for his homeland before he jumped into the back of a truck, disguised as a Soviet soldier, and fled to Italy in January 1949. Banned by FIFA after Hungarian protests, Kubala was invited to join the all-conquering Grande Torino side flying to Lisbon for a friendly against Benfica in May 1949. However, his son was ill so he stayed at home and thus wasn't killed in the Superga air disaster.

In Italy, desperate to play football, Kubala formed a team of Hungarian exiles and, on a tour of Spain, impressed Real Madrid president Santiago Bernabéu. Kubala said he would sign for the *Blancos* if his father-in-law Ferdinand Daucik became coach. In the event, Daucik ended up coaching Barcelona and Kubala followed him to Catalonia. Acquiring Spanish citizenship, Kubala made his debut for his third footballing nation in July 1953. He scored 11 goals in 19 games for Spain, but played his last international in April 1961, missing out on the World Cup in Chile.

So Kubala is the only player officially recognised to have played for three countries. And unofficially, the tally is four. Kubala also played four games for Catalonia, a footballing identity FIFA does not recognise. But whether three or four, this is a record nobody can take away from the man whom supporters, in a 1999 poll, chose as the greatest player to wear the Barcelona shirt. He is commemorated by a statue outside the Camp Nou.

🌑 Which player has been capped in the most positions?

'**Mr Versatility**, a centre-half by trade, he always gave everything, wherever he was played, centre-half or right-half, right or left full-back, he often played in goal as well and not just for the craic.' When Peter Goulding, of Football Poets, paid tribute to Irish footballer Cornelius (Con) Joseph Martin he wasn't taking any licence.

Consider the facts: Martin scored four goals in three internationals playing as a centre-forward, was bought by Aston Villa as a centre-half, played at inside-forward for Leeds United and rejected a bid from Manchester United because they wanted him in goal. There seemed no end to Martin's versatility: he played for Ireland and Northern Ireland and also won honours in Gaelic football.

He made his debut for Ireland in goal on a tour of Iberia in 1946 and scored six goals – four from the penalty spot – in 30 internationals. Though his preferred position was centre-half, Martin led the attack, and helped out at full-back and in goal when called upon. One of his penalties was scored against England at Goodison Park on 21 September 1949 when Ireland won 2-0, inflicting England's first defeat on home soil by a foreign team. Con was playing for Villa at the time and, after this historic result, got a lift back on the England team bus to Birmingham.

Belgium's bespectacled midfielder Armand Joseph 'Jef' Jurion was even more versatile, playing in seven different positions for Belgium in the 1950s. Yet neither he nor Martin covered as many positions as the legendary Austrian Gerhard Hanappi who represented his country in every position except goalkeeper.

Mr Utility, Gerhard Hanappi, at the Rapid Vienna stadium, 1961.

Hanappi made his international debut in 1948 when he was 19 as a right-half (and would not miss any of the next 55 internationals, an Austrian record) but was signed by Rapid Vienna to link defence and attack, which is why he was usually described as a centre-half. 'Signed' is probably not the right word. Hanappi desperately wanted to join Rapid, Austria's most famous working-class club, in 1950 but his club, Wacker Vienna, didn't want to sell him. So Hanappi disappeared. He claimed to have been kidnapped by Rapid's director of football Franz Binder and didn't show up for six months until Wacker relented. Yet during those 'lost' months, national coach Walter Nausch kept calling him up for international duty – and fielding him in all kinds of positions.

'He can play everywhere,' Nausch liked to say about Hanappi. This was no exaggeration. Hanappi scored 21 goals for Rapid in the 1952–53 season, a haul that made him the club's second-best forward; but he played at left-back for the Europe XI which faced England at Wembley in October 1953, marginalising the great Sir Stanley Matthews.

Hanappi's versatility didn't just extend to the pitch. A poor working-class boy who grew up with his aunt after his mother had died young, Hanappi studied architecture and designed Rapid's new stadium in the early 1970s. After he succumbed to cancer in 1980, the ground he had built was renamed Gerhard Hanappi Stadium. A footballer who could cover any outfield position and design his own stadium – that's what you call a utility player.

Have outfield players worn No. 1?

Dutch striker Ruud Geels enjoyed a long career, winning 20 caps for his country, but Netherlands coach Rinus Michels denied him his chance to make history. For the 1974 World Cup, the Dutch did not assign shirt numbers the normal way – 1 for goalkeeper, 2 for left-back and so on – but instead alphabetically. (The exception was Johan Cruyff, who demanded his customary 14.) Under this system, Geels was given the No. 1 shirt – but Michels refused to play him. There was no place in the world of Total Football for a goal machine whose greatest gift was his ability to head the ball. By the time Geels got his chance, at the 1976 European Championships, the Dutch had reverted to the normal system and he wore No. 13.

Such eccentricity wasn't unique to the Dutch. At the 1974 World Cup, Argentina allocated shirt numbers alphabetically, but made an exception by reserving numbers 1, 12 and 21 for the goalkeepers. Then four years later, as World Cup hosts, Argentina went all the way. River Plate midfielder Norberto 'Beto' Alonso wore 1, Osvaldo Ardiles 2, substitute goalkeeper Hector Baley 3 and so on. Argentina's coach Cesar Luis Menotti didn't really rate Alonso (and may have called him into the squad partly due to pressure from the junta), but he brought him on in the first group game, against Hungary, with fifteen minutes left, treating the world to the spectacle of an offensive midfielder wearing the No. 1. (At his club Alonso wore the iconic No. 10 with pride.)

There is nothing in the rules to stop an outfield player wearing No. 1, so Argentina used their system again for the 1982 and 1986 World Cups. They made exceptions for such stars as Diego Maradona, Daniel Passarella and Jorge Valdano but Ardiles didn't mind being No. 1 in 1982.

Though numbers no longer rigidly define the wearer's roles, it is rare to see an outfield player donning the No. 1 shirt. Yet in 2000, Aberdeen's Moroccan striker Hicham Zerouaki wore No. 0 after being nicknamed 'Zero' by Dons fans. The Scottish FA outlawed the number after the season was over. That was not the end of the zero shirt, however: in 2006, LA Galaxy keeper Steve Cronin adopted zero.

The Scottish FA were not the first members of the football bureaucracy to limit a player's freedom of choice. In the 1990s, Finnish midfielder Mika Lehkosuo wore 96.2 – the FM frequency of a local radio station. When HJK Helsinki qualified for the UEFA Champions League, Lehkosuo was told that UEFA only allowed players to choose from 1 to 99. He chose 96.

The Asian Football Confederation is more dogmatic, stipulating that players keep the shirt number they are given at the start of an Asian Cup qualifying campaign. This meant that winger Tommy Oar, who was obviously a long way from being the first name on Australia coach Pim Verbeek's team-sheet for the qualifiers for the 2011 Asian Cup, made his debut in a 1-0 victory against Indonesia in March 2010 with No. 121 on his back.

⚽ Which player has had the most elaborate pre-match ritual?

Putting your shirt on last (Paul Ince), placing your boots under a bust of your dad on matchday (Cristiano Ronaldo) and filling up with petrol at the same station even when you know you have enough fuel to drive home from the match (Pepe Reina), all look pretty humdrum when you consider the elaborate series of rituals with which Newcastle United striker John Tudor protected himself against ill fortune on a matchday in the 1970s.

Here is a snapshot of his typical matchday from the *Rough Guide Newcastle United 11* book: 'The striker always had lunch at noon. Always the same lunch – beans on toast and a drop of rice pudding. On the coach, he had to have a piece of spearmint gum unwrapped and given to him personally by the physio Alec Mutch. This gum was chewed throughout the game and only removed after the final whistle. Nearing the dressing room he had to have a slug of whisky – again handed to him by Mutch. Then, with striker Malcolm Macdonald, he would open a large tin of elastoplast, and use all the plaster to strap his ankles tightly. Supermac would take the empty tin, fill it with water, take out his four front false teeth, put them in the tin, close the lid and then put the tin away.' Only after this rigmarole had been completed did Tudor consider himself ready for kick-off.

⚽ Who was the first Scotsman to score in a World Cup finals?

Not Jimmy Murray, though the Hearts striker did score Scotland's first goal in the finals – to earn a 1-1 draw with Yugoslavia in 1958 in Sweden. The honour instead belongs to another Edinburghian forward, Bart McGhee, who scored the USA's first goal in a 4-0 victory over Belgium in Montevideo on 13 July 1930.

Born on 30 April 1899, McGhee was the son of James McGhee, a prolific inside-forward for Hibernian who won one cap for Scotland and managed Hearts. He suspended

Legendary Scottish winger Bart McGhee (left) playing for the USA against Argentina in the 1930 World Cup.

the club's star player Bobby Walker for missing a game and when the board sided with the Hearts star, quit and emigrated to the USA where, in 1912, his sons Bart and Jimmy joined him.

Bart shone on the wing for such picturesquely named clubs as New York Shipbuilding, Fleisher Yarn and Indiana Flooring and was playing for the New York Nationals when he was called up into the US squad for the first World Cup. An ever present as the Americans topped their group and reached the semi-finals (where they were thrashed 6-1 by Argentina) McGhee, who was 31 when the finals finished, never won another cap after the tournament was over.

The end of this pioneering Scot's career is shrouded in the fog of the Great Depression – when the game's statistics suddenly became sketchy – and a dispute between the American Soccer League and the US FA about fixtures which ultimately finished off the League. McGhee is officially credited with 137 goals in nine seasons with US clubs. Although McGhee didn't die until 1979, it isn't clear where or when he played his last competitive football. We do know it wasn't Hull City. Despite persistent reports linking him with the Tigers, his son Ed insisted that Bart had only left the US once – to represent his adopted country in Uruguay.

● Who is the most travelled player?

Long after memories of John 'Budgie' Burridge turning out for Wolves with a Superman outfit under his kit have faded, this eccentric, nomadic, goalkeeper's legend will endure in the record books because he has played for more English league clubs – fifteen, count 'em! – than any other footballer.

Those fifteen were: Workington Town (1969–71), Blackpool (1971–75), Aston Villa (1975–78), Southend United

(1977–78), Crystal Palace (1978–80), Queen's Park Rangers (1980–82), Wolves (1982–84), Derby County (1984), Sheffield United (1984–87), Southampton (1987–89), Newcastle United (1989–91), Scarborough (1993), Lincoln City (1993–94), Manchester City (1994–95) and Darlington (1995–96). Burridge's wanderlust was so great that he also played for five Scottish teams: Aberdeen, Dumbarton, Falkirk, Hibernian and Queen of the South. Since hanging up his gloves, he has become a pundit-cum-goalkeeping coach in the Middle East where he mentored Omani goalkeeper Ali Al-Habsi, who made his name at Wigan Athletic and once declared 'after God, John Burridge is the main person.'

Yet Burridge looks distinctly unadventurous when you consider goalkeeping's Phileas Fogg, Lutz Pfannenstiel. The German keeper may look like he would rather have been a wrestler, rock musician or porn star than a footballer but he has the unique distinction of being the only man to have played professionally in all six FIFA football continents: Africa, Asia, Europe, Oceania, North America and South America.

A German Under-17 international, Pfannenstiel's career started unremarkably enough at local Bavarian side Bad Kötzting in 1990. But three years later, aged 20, he signed for the Malaysian League's Penang state side, a surprising sideways move that set the nomadic precedent for the decades ahead. In 20 years between the sticks, Pfannenstiel has been on the books of (or played for) at least 27 clubs in 14 countries, completing his set of FIFA continents with spells at the Orlando Pirates (Africa), Dunedin Technical (Oceania), Calgary Mustangs (North America) and Atlético Ibirama (South America).

With the kind of plucky resolve hitherto associated with unflappable nineteenth-century explorers, Pfannenstiel has kept goal in Albania, Armenia and Namibia and been jailed on suspicion of match fixing in Singapore – even though he

Lutz Pfannenstiel finds his true home, Global United, set up to raise awareness of climate change. 'We love football, we love the planet' is their slogan.

won the games in question. (He was charged, bizarrely, with keeping goal 'suspiciously well'. Strangely, but in the circumstances understandably, Pfannenstiel denied this and the case never came to court.) He has also had run-ins with Ukrainian gangsters, which is why he prefers not to reveal which clubs he played for in that country.

Pfannenstiel – the name translates as 'panhandle' – never really made it in any of Europe's biggest leagues. A reserve keeper at Nottingham Forest from 1995 to 1997 (his nickname, predictably, was 'The German') Pfannenstiel was invariably loaned out. He is best remembered in England for having to be given the kiss of life after he stopped breathing three times while playing for Bradford Park Avenue in 2002.

Two years later, at the age of 31, he impressed AC Milan but was promptly loaned to the Calgary Mustangs. Pfannenstiel felt most at home in Norway – 'to relax and fish in a mild Norwegian summer is a dream' – where he had four spells at three clubs and came to regard Second Division side Baerum as a second home.

After hanging up his boots, Pfannenstiel formed a club, called Global United FC, which plays charity games in order to, as the team's badge says, 'fight global warming'. In March 2012, Pfannenstiel lived in an igloo for five days to raise awareness. One of the few people alive who can authoritatively make such a comparison, he insists that living in an igloo is preferable to a prison cell in Singapore. Now a scout for Hoffenheim, Pfannenstiel says: 'I don't think anyone will break this record because there aren't many people as crazy as me.'

⚽ Has any footballer ever played two matches on the same day?

On 27 January 1957, midfielder Can Bartu made a strange kind of history, scoring twice as Fenerbahçe beat Beyoğluspor 4-0 before scoring ten points in a 44-43 victory for the sports club's basketball team. Bartu had initially made his name on the basketball court but when he decided, at the age of 21, to focus all his energies on football, he was good enough to win 28 caps for Turkey and spent six profitable seasons in Serie A in the 1960s, probably the best league in the world at that time.

If you're looking for players who've starred in two football matches on the same day, three names stand out – and two of them, by a bizarre coincidence, played for Bayern Munich.

On 13 November 1985, Søren Lerby played 58 minutes as Denmark beat the Republic of Ireland 4-1 in a World Cup qualifier in Dublin. After leaving the pitch, he took a private jet back to Munich to play, as a substitute, in a German Cup match which Bayern drew 1-1 with Bochum. Almost two years to the day, Bayern organised another private jet so that Mark Hughes could play for Wales, who lost 2-0 to Czechoslovakia in Prague, and still be back in time to help Bayern beat Borussia Mönchengladbach 3-2 in a cup replay.

Mexican keeper Jorge Campos represented LA Galaxy and Mexico on the same day on 16 June 1996. The flamboyant goalie, famous for designing his own colourful kits, didn't have to leave California to double up. It was probably worth the effort because Mexico's 2-2 draw with the USA was enough to win them the US Cup for the first time.

Yet Chris Balderstone probably surpasses Bartu, Campos, Hughes and Lerby. One of England's great cricketing footballers, Balderstone made 51 not out for Leicestershire against Derbyshire in Chesterfield on 15 September 1975 before jumping into a taxi to head to Doncaster Rovers' Belle Vue ground for an evening kick-off against Brentford. After a 1-1 draw with the Bees, he was back at the crease the next day. Not content with his innings of 116 runs, the versatile 35-year-old took three wickets for 28 runs as Leicestershire wrapped up their first-ever County Championship.

Balderstone was not the first man to achieve this double and become a champion. On 30 August 1920, fast bowler Jack Durston represented Middlesex against Surrey at Lords. But he was excused fielding duties so he could keep a clean sheet for Brentford in a 1-0 victory over Millwall, in the second Football League match in the Bees' history. The next day, he took the wicket of Surrey captain Percy Fender as Middlesex won the match and the County Championship.

🌑 Did any one player win the World Cup single handedly?

'Football is a game of individuals,' one French international told football writer Philippe Auclair. A zillion motivation experts may have assured us that there is no 'I' in team (although there is a 'me'), but World Cups are often decided by the intervention of a genius. Just think about the contributions made by Garrincha (in 1962), Pelé (1970), Zizou (1998) or even Paolo Rossi (1982). And then consider the decisive intervention of Diego Maradona in 1986.

The abiding memories of that World Cup are two goals by Maradona: the brilliant, criminal improvisation of the Hand of God against England and the divine feet with which, four minutes later, he runs from his own half, leaving Peter Reid panting behind him, cuts inside Terry Butcher, touches the ball past Terry Fenwick in such a way that, as Rob Smyth noted, 'it takes Fenwick out of the game before he even knows he's in it', and slides the ball past Peter Shilton into the net.

For Maradona's team-mate Jorge Valdano, the goal symbolised El Diego's 'personal journey'. It looked like a once-in-a-lifetime goal but four days later, albeit from a more central position further up the field, he scored with a carbon copy run against Belgium in the semi-final. That slalom may have been inspired by the memory of Belgian keeper Jean-Marie Pfaff's pre-tournament verdict on the little No. 10. 'Maradona,' Pfaff had insisted, 'is nothing special.'

Apart from those three goals what did he do? Well, he scored five and was credited with five assists – one of them being the winner in the final. So he played a part in ten of the 14 goals Argentina scored in the finals. His other stats aren't bad either: he embarked on 90 dribbles (three times as

Diego Maradona skips past Terry Butcher and Peter Shilton points the way to eternal glory.

many as any of his team-mates), won 53 free-kicks (more than twice as many as any team-mate) and attempted or set up over half his side's shots. No wonder he won the Golden Ball with 1,281 votes, with Harald Schumacher, who had made such an indelible impression on Patrick Battiston in 1982, a distant second on 344. (A bizarre postscript to this vote: the trophy presented to Maradona was later stolen while on tour and melted down into gold bars on the orders of a mafia don.)

Argentina, mind you, were not a one-man team. Striker Valdano, midfielders Sergio Batista and Jorge Burruchaga, and defenders Daniel Passarella and Oscar Ruggeri were all considerable talents. Indeed, coach Oscar Bilardo's side were so efficient at the back that they only conceded five goals, keeping three clean sheets in seven games. Yet Bilardo, who changed his tactics to give Maradona a free-floating role as the second striker from the quarter-finals onwards, certainly did his utmost to build the team around a footballer who was easily the greatest player in the world at that time.

You can imagine Brazil still winning without Pelé in 1970 (as they had in 1962). It's harder to envisage France still triumphing in 1998 without Zizou. But it is impossible to conceive of Argentina winning in 1986 without the transcendental, game-changing genius that was Diego Armando Maradona in his prime. As an enraptured Clive Gammon wrote in *Sports Illustrated*: 'How many games can a single genius win on his own? As many as he needs to.'

Gaffers

🌐 **Who was the first coach to discover the importance of diet?**

In October 1996, Arsenal players staged the great Mars bar revolt. Travelling away to Blackburn for their first match under new coach Arsène Wenger, the players at the back of the bus began chanting: 'We want our Mars bars!' The aforementioned items of confectionery, hitherto a staple of the team's matchday diet, had been banned by their French coach on the grounds that: 'I find it stupid that a player can practice all week and spoil his game because he eats something silly 24 hours before.' Wenger didn't back down, telling his players: 'Food is like kerosene. If you put the wrong one in your car, it's not as quick as it should be.'

At the time, Wenger's views on diet – along with his insistence on improving the dressing rooms' feng shui and pre-match muscle-honing stretches – led a credulous British media to position him as the latest in a grand Gallic tradition of scientific pioneers that stretched back to Marie Curie and Louis Pasteur. Yet he was far from the first coach to realise that there was a connection between a footballer's diet and their performance.

The same thought had occurred to the Chilean World Cup squad in 1962. Food and drink formed a central part of their pre-match preparation, albeit not in a way Wenger would have understood. The hosts of the 1962 mundial ate cheese before their opening game against Switzerland (which they won 3-1), tucked into spaghetti on the eve of their clash with Italy (which they won, controversially, 2-0) and downed vodka before they overcame USSR 2-1 in the quarter-finals. Chile then succumbed to Brazil in the semi-finals possibly because their pre-match sampling of their opponents' cuisine was restricted to a few cups of coffee.

One of the USSR stars to miss out on a place in the 1962 World Cup was winger Valeriy Lobanovskiy. A supreme individualist as a player, Lobanovskiy became, as Dynamo Kiev coach, an influential advocate of a scientific, systematic approach to the game that regarded players as components, not people. As components, they had to be in perfect condition so he insisted his players follow a strict dietary regime.

Lobanovskiy's dietary regime was following in the footsteps of one of European football's greatest autocrats, Helenio Herrera. In the 1960s, the Argentine mastermind of the all-conquering *Nerazzurri* side known as Grande Inter had given players their own diet sheets and forbidden them from smoking or drinking 'super-alcolici' (a blend of whisky and grappa). To make it easier to enforce these rules, Herrera

No Mars bars for the boys. Britain's favourite nutty professor, Arsène Wenger, chews the cud with the then England manager, Sven Goran Eriksson.

insisted his players prepared for a game by getting together for a *ritiro* (retreat).

Yet decades before Herrera laid down the law, a revolutionary, detailed approach to diet and training helped Tom Watson win the English league at Sunderland (1892, 1893 and 1895) and Liverpool (1901). The players' day started at 7.30am with a stroll, breakfast at 8.30am ideally consisted of weak tea, chops, eggs, dry toast or stale bread. Training started at 9.45am and again at 3.30pm. A glass of beer or claret was recommended at dinner, during which tobacco could be 'sparingly used'. The players then rounded off the day at 7.30pm with an hour's stroll.

As unscientific as all this may sound, it certainly marks a step forward from the dietary regime Blackburn Olympic laid down for their players before the 1883 FA Cup final. As Hunter Davies recalls in *Boots, Balls And Haircuts*, 'Their diet consisted of a glass of port wine at six in the morning, followed by two raw eggs and walk along the sands. For breakfast they had porridge and haddock. Lunch was a leg of mutton. Tea was more porridge and a pint of milk. Supper was a dozen oysters each. It seemed to work. They beat the Old Etonians 2-1.'

In such a context, Watson's views were nothing less than revolutionary. Ninety years before Wenger famously complained that the British diet contained too much sugar and not enough vegetables, sugar was one of the ingredients – along with butter, milk and potatoes – that Watson urged his players to avoid.

⚽ Who was the best-dressed coach?

Clothes maketh the manager. They were certainly central to the aura that surrounded Mourinho when he arrived at Stamford Bridge in 2004, with his couture suits and shirts, top button undone and tie slightly askew. The Portuguese coach's Armani overcoat came to symbolise his distinctive style, inspiring a cult T-shirt (with the words 'Mourinho's coat' emblazoned across the top) and famously fetching around £22,000 at a charity auction.

On his return to the Premier League, Mourinho has dressed more soberly, almost as if he's signalling his desire to focus on the serious business at hand. His toughest competition in the best dressed stakes is probably his old protégé, André Villas-Boas, although the Spurs manager lost points on style when he was spotted wearing a thermal vest under his tasteful dark suit. Both fare better than Arsenal boss Arsène Wenger whose elongated parka has been likened to a Michelin Man and has inspired a Facebook page 'Buy Arsène Wenger a New Coat'.

Style had not previously been the buzzword among coaches in England's Premier League, who had, according to Sarah Lyall in the *New York Times*, traditionally gravitated towards three looks: Italian playboy, 1970s East German apparatchik, and slob in tracksuit. But it had not always been thus. In 1970, Vic Buckingham, the debonair, eccentric, much-travelled English coach, who had managed West Brom to victory in the 1954 FA Cup and given a promising 19-year-old called Johan Cruyff his Ajax debut, took over at Barcelona. As Jimmy Burns recounts in his book, *La Roja*: 'He liked to dress in tweed jackets and silk ties and, in the winter months, a beige button-down jersey.' His demeanour and his liking for cocktails, golf and horseracing led some Catalans to see him as a cross between a retired Army officer and Henry Higgins.

The Higgins look was Buckingham's more flamboyant, upwardly mobile take on a style that Barney Ronay identified in his book *The Absurd Ascent Of The Most Important Man In Football*, as 'the uniform of the universal dad', as exemplified by the Crombie overcoat, trilby and pipe worn by Sir Matt Busby, presenting United's legendary boss as, in Ronay's words 'a prosperous small-town sawmill and wood chippings magnate.' This approach began to look outmoded in the 1960s when Alf Ramsey won the World Cup wearing a tracksuit, although in the public eye he was synonymous with the brown raincoat he so often wore. After the social revolution that swept through Britain in the 1960s, many managers wore tracksuits because it gave the impression that they were hands-on types who were closer to their players. The change in fashion even swayed Busby who mused, when he retired in 1969, that it might be 'time for a younger tracksuited man to take over'. Yet other coaches stood out from the crowd: Malcolm Allison was flamboyant in a fedora, John Bond looked like a TV cop (albeit not a very exciting one) in his trench coat and, by the end of the 1970s, Ron Atkinson was styling himself as the Thatcherite king of bling.

In many countries, tracksuited coaches had already made their mark. When West Germany won the 1954 World Cup, their manager Sepp Herberger was wearing a trench coat to protect him from the rain but he wore a tracksuit under that and rounded off the ensemble with adidas sports shoes. This look would inspire generations of German coaches, most notably Otto Rehhagel who won Euro 2004 with Greece. Herberger felt so at ease in his tracksuit that, according to a 1996 biography of the great man, he was buried in it.

Yet today, the tracksuit has fallen out of fashion, possibly because its mystique was destroyed by the Graham Taylor documentary *Do I Not Like That*. When Owen Coyle wears one he looks like he's trying to kid his team, the fans and himself that if all else fails he can run on to the pitch and sort it out. Most managers in Europe prefer the gravitas of suits, especially if they don't have any gravitas of their own. Italian coaches like Luciano Spalletti have shown that a really good coat is almost as important as a coaching badge.

Yet enterprising coaches can still make a statement on the touchline. Hervé Renard, the Frenchman who won the 2012 African Cup of Nations with Zambia, usually patrols the touchline in straight-leg jeans and an untucked white shirt. Although he resembled a member of a 1990s boy band, his look was certainly more successful than the flowery shirts Dunga wore as Brazil coach, or Tony Pulis's disconcerting combo of tracksuit and baseball cap.

Joachim Löw and Hans-Dieter Flick in their matching cobalt blue cashmere jumpers at the 2010 World Cup. Probably not a look suited to Roy Hodgson.

The cobalt cashmere V-neck sweaters worn by Germany coach Joachim Löw and his assistant Hans-Dieter Flick during the 2010 World Cup struck such a chord back home that upscale clothier Strenesse sold out of them. Some desperate fans even drove to the Netherlands to snap up a Jogi sweater. These V-necks may be the most distinctive good luck charms worn in the dugout since Allison's fedora. Yet by Euro 2012, perhaps disappointed that the allegedly lucky blue V-necks had taken Germany only to third place in South Africa, Löw and Flick had settled for white shirts and grey suits.

⚽ Who led the most dysfunctional World Cup campaign ever?

There's major competition here but three ill-fated World Cup campaigns spring immediately to mind: Germany's in 1938, Scotland's in 1978 and France's in 2010. And, naturally, the blame for each would rest with their managers.

Austria and Germany had both qualified for the 1938 World Cup in France. Yet after the *Anschluss*, in which Nazi Germany annexed Adolf Hitler's homeland, it was decided that only one team would enter the finals. (Sweden benefitted from this decision with a late call-up.) Felix Linnemann, head of the German FA, explained the rationale to coach Sepp Herberger: 'In our sphere as well as in the others, a visible expression of our solidarity with the Austrians who have come back to the Reich has to be presented.' The Führer demanded a 6:5 or 5:6 ratio between German and Austrian players in the team.

This was easy to say, harder to do. For a start, how do you unite a squad of 22 players around a common cause, when nine of the players are from a country that has just been annexed/invaded by the country the other 13 are from? Especially when three of the nine Austrians in Germany's 1938 World Cup squad played for Austria Vienna, whose captain Karl Musch would have to emigrate because his wife was Jewish.

The players didn't just belong to different countries, they had graduated from different football schools. Still in thrall to the legend of their sublime, free-flowing Wunderteam, the Austrians were steeped in a Vienna coffee-house view of football which saw the game as a cerebral contest, in which players must out-think, out-pass, out-play the opposition. The Germans had their own great side to revere, known as the Breslau-Elf, an exhilarating amalgam of direct English play, Scottish passing

Swiss football's finest hour, as Hitler's Germany-Austria head home from the World Cup in 1938.

game and the Danubian style. Named after the city in which they beat Denmark 8-0 in May 1937, Herberger's scintillating side won ten out of eleven games in 1937.

Herberger knew that reconciling all these factors was going to be like squaring the circle, but he tried. He arranged a practice match to, as he noted, 'get the Austrians down from their heaven of supposed superiority'. The session degenerated into a keepy-uppy contest between Viennese star Josef Stroh and Schalke's Fritz Szepan that ended with the German midfielder volleying the ball against the wall just over the Austrian players' heads and whispering, 'You arseholes.'

Despite Herberger's entreaties, Austria's best player, Matthias Sindelar, opted out of the tournament, insisting he was unfit. So with 13 Germans, nine Austrians, and two keepy-uppy kings, Herberger set off for France. The campaign kicked off against Switzerland, a country which had come to fiercely dislike its growing Fascist neighbour. Though Germany took the lead through Josef Gauchel, Switzerland equalised and it became clear that, as journalist Christian Eichler put it, 'Germans and Austrians prefer to play against each other even when they're in the same team'. In the replay five days Germany went 2-0 up and were on track for victory until the Swiss grabbed three goals in the last 26 minutes to win 4-2. For the one and only time in the history of the World Cup, Germany were out in the first round.

Fast forward 40 years to 1978 and a Scotland team facing pressures created largely by their coach Ally MacLeod, who declared: 'You can mark down 25 June 1978 as the day Scottish football conquered the world. For on that Sunday, I'm convinced the finest team this country has ever produced can play in the final of the World Cup in Buenos Aires and win.' Asked what he planned to do after winning the World Cup, MacLeod said: 'Retain it.' Even for a coach who had begun his first press conference as Scotland coach with the words 'My name is Ally MacLeod and I am a winner', this was a bit much. However, 30,000 supporters paid to cheer off their departing heroes at Hampden Park, prompting Lou Macari to remark later: 'You don't normally have a victory parade before a ball is even kicked.'

The flames were soon dampened by Scotland's performances on the pitch. Footballers are a superstitious bunch, always looking out for omens, and the sight of two dead horses on the road to the team's training ground in Cordoba must have seemed inauspicious. They also realised, as soon as the aircraft doors opened in Buenos Aires, that Argentina was hot.

Still, against Peru they played well only to lose 3-1, undone primarily by the brilliance of Teófilo Cubillas. This might have seemed a useful reality check but worse was to follow. Winger Willie Johnston failed a drug test after taking Reactivan, a mild stimulant to combat hay fever, and was sent home. As social historian Dominic Sandbrook put it: 'Scotland's march of destiny was beginning to look more like a night at the circus.'

Against Iran, Scotland played like clowns, scraping a 1-1 draw after Iranian left-back Andranik Eskandarian sliced the ball into his own net. The Scotland team had to run a gauntlet of V-sign flicking, tam-o'shanter-wearing supporters as they left the pitch. In Dundee, a record shop cut the price of 'Ally's Tartan Army' singles to 1p, inviting customers to buy as many as they wanted and smash them to pieces with a hammer on the counter. Even the magnificent 3-2 win over the Netherlands – and a sublime slalom by Archie Gemmill to score the greatest goal of his career – couldn't redeem this campaign. In the *Observer*, Hugh McIlvanney, a proud but humiliated Scot, said that in the run-up to the finals MacLeod 'behaved with no more caution, subtlety or concern for planning than a man ready to lead a bayonet charge'.

When the players returned to Glasgow Airport, they were jeered by baggage handlers. Some say the sudden, stunning revelation of the nation's footballing inadequacy accounted for Scotland's failure to endorse devolution in the 1979 referendum. Be that as it may, the Scottish Football Blog probably summed it up best: 'Football was creating a global village. Scotland would provide the idiot.'

Yet the travails of Germany and Scotland pale into insignificance compared to the agonies of France's 2010 World Cup campaign during which – and these are just the edited highlights – Nicolas Anelka was sent home for using the half-time interval to tell beleaguered coach Raymond

Raymond Domenech is escorted from the pitch by the fouth official and referee during the 2010 FIFA World Cup match with Uruguay.

Domenech to 'go and get yourself fucked up your arse, you and your tactics', the players went on strike for a training session in protest at his punishment, and Franck Ribéry had to appear on national television to deny, not terribly convincingly, that he had plotted against French playmaker Yoann Gourcuff.

The first World Cup strike was, as Philippe Auclair points out in his biography of Thierry Henry, 'nothing more than a symbolic downing of tools in a Sunday morning training session'. Still, as Auclair noted, there was a certain irony in the fact that the pitch in Knysna the players weren't training on – in front of a few hundred local children – was called the Field Of Dreams. On this evocatively named piece of turf, skipper Patrice Evra and fitness coach Robert Duverne almost came to blows. Duverne and goalkeeping coach Bruno Martin were, Auclair reports, 'later seen in tears, hidden behind a lorry, a few paces away from the bus where the mutineers had barricaded themselves (and on whose sides this slogan could be read: 'All together towards a new blue dream')'.

The results were almost as unedifying: les Bleus suffered their first-ever defeats to Mexico and South Africa (after the latter game, in which Gourcuff was sent off, Domenech mysteriously refused to shake hands with South Africa coach Carlos Alberto Parreira), won just one point, and scored only one goal as they finished bottom of Group A.

The only appropriate way to end such a campaign – which started with the symbolically prophetic image of William Gallas crashing his dune-buggy in pre-tournament training and ended with sports minister Roselyne Bachelot calling the team a 'moral disaster' – was for president Nicolas Sarkozy to hold an inquest at the Champs Élysées palace with Thierry Henry. By the time the dust had settled, Domenech had been replaced by Laurent Blanc, four players (Anelka, Ribéry, Evra and Jeremy Toulalan) were banned for varying numbers of matches, Henry had retired from international football and Jean-Pierre Escalettes had quit as president of the French FA.

Le Parisien caught France's national mood rather well by noting, 'To have the worst team at the World Cup was unbearable. To also have the most stupid is intolerable.'

🌐 Who was England's first manager?

Walter Winterbottom was the first man to be permanently given the title of England manager but he was also director of coaching at the FA and didn't usually do the one thing every modern manager insists on: picking the team. That job was given to a select committee of FA blazers and, as Barney Ronay notes in *The Manager*, in 139 matches in charge, the donnish Winterbottom had sole responsibility for picking the team just once: in October 1959, for a friendly against Sweden at Wembley. Given the historic nature of this selection, it's perhaps worth listing that XI: Eddie Hopkinson, Don Howe, Tony Allen, Ronnie Clayton (captain), Trevor Smith, Ron Flowers, John Connelly, Brian Clough (winning his second, and last, cap for England), Jimmy Greaves, Bobby Charlton and Edwin Holliday. Sweden won 3-2. True, the Swedes had reached the World Cup final in 1958, but giving Winterbottom sole charge had hardly proved an unqualified success.

The first full-time England boss to pick his own team was Sir Alf Ramsey. Yet he only secured that right after the committee's disastrous selection for his first match, against France in a freezing Paris in February 1963, led to a 5-2 defeat. Afterwards, Ramsey asked England captain Jimmy Armfield: 'Do we always play like that?' 'No,' said Armfield. 'That's the first good news I've had all evening,' replied Ramsey. By the time the 1966 World Cup started, Sir Alf was the undisputed master of team selection.

Yet neither Ramsey nor Winterbottom were the first managers of England. Ronay says the great Herbert Chapman became 'the first de facto England manager' in 1933. The Arsenal coach gave the pre-match tactical team talk, helped organise the side that drew 1-1 with Italy in Rome and lost the keys to the dressing room at half-time.

Herbert Chapman on a scouting trip to Vienna in 1932, in preparation for England international duties.

Vittorio Pozzo, Chapman's friend and rival, was surprised to see the Arsenal boss emerging from England's dressing room. When asked what he was doing in Rome, Chapman told Pozzo: 'I'm doing for my team what you are doing for yours'.' That wasn't quite true. Chapman was acting unofficially and didn't pick the team, although two Arsenal stars, Eddie Hapgood and Cliff Bastin, scorer of England's equaliser, did play. The match, the first between the *Azzurri* and the Three Lions, was played in front of 50,000 cheering fans. In the crowd was Benito Mussolini, who Hapgood hit in the midriff with a stray clearance. Il Duce dropped in to the England dressing room afterwards, Bastin recalling that the Italian dictator was so charismatic that he made Chapman seem like an 'utter nonentity'.

Writing in *The Sports Historian* in May 1996, Tony Say says that 'despite objections from selectors', Chapman 'acted as the unofficial manager to the England team' in Italy and against Switzerland in Berne when the manager's inspirational words 'helped effect a 4-0 victory over a strong Swiss team'.

Some historians have also credited Tom Whittaker, who trained the Arsenal first team under Chapman and later managed the club, as manager for six England matches, most notably in a 5-2 victory over Scotland in 1930. But the evidence that his influence extended beyond training is not compelling. So it seems most likely that Chapman was, as Ronay suggests, England's first gaffer.

⚽ Who has coached the most national teams?

Carlos Alberto Parreira and Bora Milutinović may jointly hold the record for coaching five teams in World Cup finals, but that isn't that impressive when you consider the career of a man who made the Guinness Book of World Records well over a decade ago, has published three autobiographies to date, and is known as the 'Hemingway of Football' for his countless tales of woe and wonder. Oh, and Rudi Gutendorf has coached 55 teams in 30 countries on five continents, among them 18 national teams. (That figure rises to 20 if you add the Olympic teams of Iran and China, which Gutendorf managed for the 1988 and 1992 Games, respectively.)

If he's so ubiquitous, how come you have never heard of him? Probably because he hasn't won very much. Gutendorf coached Duisburg to a sensational runners-up spot in the Bundesliga in 1964 (see 'Who invented Total Football?') and Schalke to the Cup Winners' Cup semi-finals in 1970.

But these are his only achievements in a major competition. He only actually won something in Switzerland (as player-manager of Lucerne in 1960) and Japan, where he coached Yomiuri Tokyo to the 1985 championship.

Gutendorf seldom plied his trade in the obvious places. He coached clubs in Tunisia, Tanzania, Peru and Mauritius. And if he took over a national team, it was usually a side like Fiji, Tonga, or Antigua. He came close to hitting the limelight in 1973, when his Chile side beat Peru and drew away to the USSR, qualifying for the World Cup because the Russians refused to play the second leg. But the coup d'etat that ultimately killed his friend Salvador Allende forced Gutendorf to leave Chile before the 1974 finals.

Rudi Gutendorf has another crack at glory, this time round with the Rwanda national team in 1999.

This stay in Chile is full of the kind of stories that punctuate Gutendorf's career. In his few months in the country, the then 46-year-old enjoyed an affair with a teenage Miss Chile and was shot at with a machine gun while steering his jeep through the countryside. Then he got into another affair, with a girl more than 20 years his junior. It is suspected that she was secretly working for the CIA. One night, Gutendorf and his lover were lying in bed, when a man opened the door and aimed a gun at the woman. The shot shattered Gutendorf's jawbone before hitting the woman's head, killing her instantly. He still has the scar to remind him.

Stories likes these abound in Gutendorf's autobiographies which read, at times, like magical realist novels. Yet don't be fooled: Gutendorf is no hopeless romantic – he's a fanatically determined coach. When he managed the Socceroos between 1979 and 1981, an Australian official instructed him, 'We want a coach, not a Führer.' The jibe didn't change Gutendorf's approach. As he told the *Sydney Morning Herald*, 'I can be a bastard on the field. I get too excited. I like to knife everyone when they do something I don't like. There is a saying in Germany: without sweat there is no reward.'

🌑 Who was the scariest manager?

'I ... Will ... Not ... Have ... A ... Coward ... In ... My ... Team.' That terrible chant was how Eddie Cramp remembered Stan Cullis, the former sergeant major who managed Wolves from 1948 to 1964, winning three league titles and two FA Cups. Some coaches are tactically innovative, others coax their teams into playing attractive football and a few enjoy record-breaking success. What set Cullis apart was that he, as Barney Ronay puts it in his book on managers, 'saw football as an absolute test of human endurance. Once one of his players,

THERE IS NO SUBSTITUTE FOR HARD WORK

Wolverhampton Wanderers manager Stan Cullis gives a team-talk in the dressing room. Not so much hard but fair as ... hard.

Ted Farmer, was brutally elbowed in the stomach. At half-time Farmer found he was passing blood. Cullis told the club doctor: 'Wait till it comes through his backside before you take him off.' Farmer was later diagnosed with a pierced bladder.'

To be fair to Cullis, he himself wouldn't have left the pitch with such an injury when he was a half-back. Badly concussed during the 1938–39 season, he played on, knowing that the next concussion might prove fatal, until 1947, retiring only when the doctors said just heading the ball would kill him. Installed as Wolves manager, he made his mark by introducing training sessions in which players endured commando-style assault courses and had to meet specific targets for running 100 yards, 220 yards, 440 yards, 880 yards, one mile, three miles and jump at least 4ft 9in into the air. War had taught him that, he said, 'proper training can cause the abnormal achievement to be the normal one'.

This military-style regimen was surprisingly popular in British football, reaching an absurd, but glorious, apotheosis in the 1970s when former Royal Marine Tony Toms organised training sessions when Jack Charlton was managing Sheffield Wednesday. In pre-season one summer, Toms took them to a commando base on the south coast where the players, in full military dress, were pushed into an S-bend pipe full of water before being hauled out at the other end by a team-mate. One player was heard calling for his mother. Wednesday's Yugoslav midfielder Ante Miročević looked at the pipe, asked 'Where's the ball?' and then ran off.

Yet even if you set Cullis in context, the Iron Manager still looks tougher than the rest. Other managers – notably Brian Clough's mentor Alan Brown – cheerfully perpetuated their tough guy image. ('You may have heard people say I'm a bastard,' Brown told Clough when they first met. 'Well, they're right.') Cullis instilled such terror that he had no need of such flourishes. When attacker Dennis Wilshaw was asked to explain why Wolves' team spirit remained so high, he replied: 'Because we all hated his [Cullis's] guts.'

Felix Magath must wish he had coached in Cullis's day. Nicknamed 'Quälix' (a play on his first name and *qual* or 'torture'), his remorseless efforts to instil the right kind of discipline at eight Bundesliga clubs have made him notorious. When he left Wolfsburg in October 2012, the first thing the gleeful players did was have a whipround to buy a CD player so they could play music in the dressing room again.

Magath's distinctive contribution to the coaching profession was probably his elaborate system of fines. Penalising players for being late for training is hardly unheard of but Magath's fines included €500 for letting the ball bounce in front of you and €1,000 for an unnecessary back pass. He famously fined Wolfsburg striker Patrick Helmes €10,000 for not working hard enough when the other side had possession. This unusual approach may explain why Jefferson Farfan, who played under Quälix at Schalke, said once: 'I would rather go back to Peru and break stones than play for him again.'

Yet Magath's method of instilling fear in his players often brought short-term results, which is why he was known as an unusually successful fireman, a coach brought in to ward off relegation.

Felix Magath looks set to dish out another fine at Wolfsburg.

Scots, of course, have a special place in management, most famously with Alex Ferguson's 'hairdryer' and the odd flying boot. One of his countrymen, Jimmy Sirrel, deserves a mention in dispatches, too. Between 1967 and 1982, the Scot managed Brentford, Notts County, Sheffield United and Notts County. At County, he developed the knack of identifying players' footsteps so he could tell which ones were sneaking into training late. He threatened to fine defender David McVay for growing a beard and once took on thousands of rampaging Manchester United supporters at Meadow Lane armed only with self-belief and a scalpel. Sirrel had his own way of solving such mysterious issues as loss of form. When County striker Trevor Christie stopped scoring, Sirrel walked up to Christie in the dressing room, punched him twice in the stomach and said, 'Big man, you're a fucking coward.' The striker scored twice that afternoon.

Such crude methods would have appalled Major Frank Buckley, the famous Wolves manager. When his striker Gordon Clayton hit a barren streak, Buckley sent him – at his wife's suggestion – to a psychologist. It worked: Clayton scored 14 goals in the next 15 matches.

Forever known as Major because he had commanded the Footballers' Battalion in World War I – he nearly died when shrapnel punctured his lungs – Buckley managed seven clubs between 1919 and 1955 but is best known for his 17-year stint at Wolves, where he revolutionised training and tactics, and enriched the club with his pioneering approach to the discovery, purchase and sale of football talent.

Buckley was a complex, often contradictory character who was willing to experiment with new tactics and even new drugs but treated his players as if they were soldiers in his private battalion. He didn't like them to marry as he feared it made them less focused. At Blackpool, he gave each player a little book outlining the behaviour he expected of them. After Wolves lost to Mansfield in the FA Cup, he humiliated his players by forcing them to walk through the city centre in their kit. His captain was, of course, Stan Cullis.

With a style of management that veered from benign dictatorship to malevolent dictatorship, Buckley was an obsessive, perfectionist, pseudo-scientific, micro-managing trailblazer, a precedent-setting genius whose distorted reflection can be seen in the careers of Sir Alex Ferguson, Arrigo Sacchi and José Mourinho.

In 1990 Sacchi's Milan became the last side to retain the European Cup. Though his training regime was as punishing as any devised by Buckley or Cullis, that wasn't why the *Rossoneri* were so frightened of him. As Carlo Ancelotti reveals in his memoirs, what really spooked them was the sight of Sacchi screaming and shouting in his sleep: 'He emitted terrifying sounds as if someone was cutting his throat. Every so often there would be a technical comment as well, even in his sleep. "Run diagonal!" or "Go back!" The man never stopped.'

⚽ Who had the shortest managerial career?

Leroy Rosenior is so undisputedly the record holder in this category that we have plenty of time for some honorary mentions first. No, not people like Brian Clough, whose 44 days at Leeds United was positively long-term compared to some other men who found out the hard way why they call football management the sack race.

Consider poor Alberto Malesani, who was fired by Genoa in April 2012 following a 4-1 defeat by Siena that so enraged the *tifosi* that they plastered the pitch with flares and bengal lights. When he was sacked, Malesani had been coaching the team for only 20 days. This isn't anywhere near the record but Malesani's case is worth a mention because he had already coached Genoa between June and December 2011, which means he was sacked twice in one season by the same club.

For truly short managerial reigns, you have to focus on those that didn't last even a day. Even the most ludicrously incompetent managers can't cobble together a string of poor results in just a few hours so there were all kinds of reasons for these dismissals or resignations. Pills were the undoing of Heinz Höher, a veteran German coach who had been out of a job for eight years when second-division Lübeck called him in October 1996, having fired their manager earlier that morning. Höher was so eager to revive his career, he drove to Lübeck, overseeing his first training session that very afternoon – until he suddenly lost consciousness. Officials presumed Höher had fainted but he later revealed that he had been taking medication against alcoholism and had swallowed too many pills before jumping into the car. With Höher in hospital, Lübeck began their search for a third manager that day.

In September 1998, Paul Breitner's son answered the phone, listened for a few moments and yelled: 'Dad, there's someone named Braun who wants to talk to you!' The caller was Egidius Braun, president of the German FA and he wanted to offer Breitner the post of national coach. Berti Vogts had just resigned and the mood surrounding the team was so bad that Braun felt he needed someone who would truly shake things up. Breitner's coaching experience began and ended with a local Under-10 side, but the 1974 World Cup winner had a reputation as a maverick genius. He considered the offer briefly, then said yes. A few hours later, Braun called again. 'Herr Breitner, I just want to make sure that you're not going to cop out,' he said. Breitner assured him he would stand by his word and went to bed as the new German national coach. The next morning, Braun called for the third time in 15 hours to inform Breitner that there was too much opposition within the German FA. 'I'm sorry, just forget it,' he concluded.

It took just five hours for Zbigniew Boniek to realise he was at the wrong place at the wrong time. Early in the 1991–92 season, he was asked by Pisa's long-serving president Romeo Anconetani to coach the Serie A club. On 18 September, a Wednesday, Boniek agreed to a contract and went for a celebratory dinner with Anconetani. It may have been the food, location or, as the Associated Press later reported, a disagreement over the make-up of Pisa's technical staff, but Boniek quit before the meal had finished.

However, even five hours seems like an eternity when you consider Leroy Rosenior's ten-minute tenure at Torquay. He was presented as the Gulls' new gaffer on 17 May 2007, during a press conference. While Rosenior was talking to the media, main shareholder Mike Bateson agreed to sell his stake in the club to a new consortium – and the new owners wanted a different manager. 'I did all the interviews,' Rosenior later explained. 'And within 10 minutes, Mike called me to let me know he had actually sold the club.'

This bizarre incident was widely reported, because it made Rosenior the new world-record holder. By then, he had become wearily accustomed to short periods at the helm. He had resigned as Shrewsbury Town's assistant manager after three months in 2006 and taken over at Brentford where he lasted only five months. On 7 May 2007, less than two weeks before his truncated reign at Torquay, he coached the Sierra Leone team (he had won one cap for the Leone Stars in 1994) against Leyton Orient in London, which means he was their national coach for one day.

🌑 Who was the youngest manager to win a league championship?

Trusting really young managers, with little or no previous experience in the dugout, is often imagined to be a modern phenomenon. In 2009, Josep Guardiola became, at 38, the youngest manager to win the UEFA Champions League and two years later, in 2011, the 33-year-old André Villas-Boas won the Portuguese league and then the UEFA Europa League with Porto, setting a record for both competitions. The bad news for AVB is that as much of a whippersnapper as he might seem, he is already too old to become the youngest manager to win the English title.

Tom Watson was only 33 when he won the old Division One with Sunderland in 1892. One of his secrets, contemporary accounts suggest, was his insistence that on really cold days his players should have whisky massaged into their chests and backs at half-time. By the time he turned 42, he had won the title twice more with Sunderland and once with Liverpool, establishing himself as the first great manager in the English game (an honour usually given to Herbert Chapman), before dying of pleurisy and pneumonia in 1915, at the age of 56.

Watson's success proves that club owners, presidents and directors have long been willing to hire coaches on the principle that 'if you're good enough you're old enough'. In 1956, the first European Cup was won by a legendary Real Madrid side coached by 36-year-old José Villalonga. The year before, at 35, Villalonga had won la Liga, a record that stood until 1983, when Athletic Bilbao won the Spanish title under Javier Clemente. Since the season ended on 1 May, eleven days before Clemente's birthday, he was still only 32 when he won the title. Youth in the dugout does not automatically translate to flamboyance on

José Villalonga enters Real Madrid legend, after his team came back from 2-0 down against Stade de Reims to win 3-2 and claim the European Cup in 1956.

the pitch, though. If you were a supporter, Bilbao's tackling was tenacious. Opponents, most notably Barcelona's coach Cesar Luis Menotti, found it crude. Clemente memorably dismissed Menotti as 'an ageing hippie'.

Thirty-two is very young for a championship-winning coach. In Germany, the record is held by Matthias Sammer, 34 when he won the Bundesliga with Dortmund in 2002. In Italy, Arpad Weisz was 34 when he won Serie A with Inter in 1930. In France, Albert Batteux lifted the 1953 championship with Stade de Reims, in a season that ended 39 days before Batteux turned 34.

It will take a real wunderkind to coach a championship-winning side at a younger age than Bob Houghton. He was born on 30 October 1947 – the importance of the date will become clear later – and started his playing career up front for Fulham. At only 23, he became player-manager of Hastings United, later taking the same role at Maidstone United and assisting Bobby Robson at Ipswich. In early 1974, he took over at Malmö and – as *The Guardian* said in 2006 – 'brought 4-4-2, pressing and revolutionary training techniques to the country'. The season, which follows the calendar year in Sweden, started on 13 April and ended on 27 October, three days before Houghton's birthday. Malmö finished the season top of the table, nine points ahead of AIK Solna, meaning Houghton was just 26 when he won his first league title as coach.

He won two more league titles with Malmö while he was still in his twenties. In 1979, at the age of 31, he stunned Europe by leading the Swedish side to the European Cup final. They lost 1-0 to Nottingham Forest, managed by 44-year-old Brian Clough. Houghton's coaching career has since taken him across the globe but whether he plied his trade in Bristol, India, Toronto or Uzbekistan, he has never won another league title.

Records

⚽ **Which side holds the record for away wins in a single season?**

In 2004–05, José Mourinho's Chelsea won 15 out of 19 games away from home, a Premier League record. Seven seasons later, Mourinho's Real Madrid won 16 out of 19 on the road to set a new La Liga record. Yet this record is held not by a team of galactical, multi-millionaires but by a young side scrambled together as the chaos of World War Two settled. In 1946–47, Doncaster Rovers' away record in Division Three (North) was Played 21, Won 18, Drew 1, Lost 2, Goals for/against 56/24.

That season, Rovers swept almost all before them. Home and away became almost an irrelevance – in those days of two points for a win they dropped only five on the road, compared to seven at their Belle Vue stadium. Donny scored 112 goals (a club record) and won 33 games (a club and Football League record). Clarrie Jordan, a 24-year-old striker who had shown promise up front for Upton Colliery during World War II, banged in 42 goals in one season (also a club record), registered three hat-tricks and scored for ten games in a row. That was as good as it got for Jordan who retired in 1954, after a career blighted by the wrong move (to Sheffield Wednesday) injuries and loss of form; he later ran a pub in Doncaster.

What was the greatest comeback?

'Greatest comeback' depends to a large degree on the definition of 'great'. Is it the occasion, the deficit, the circumstances, the time left on the clock, or a combination of all these and more? On several of these counts, it will remain hard to outdo Liverpool, who won the 2005 UEFA Champions League after trailing Milan 3-0 at half-time. At stake, after all, was the biggest trophy in club football and the opponents were Italians, not known for throwing away leads. Then again, does a comeback have to mean a big deficit? What of Manchester United's return from the dead in the 1999 final against Bayern Munich, turning 1-0 at 90 minutes into 2-1 at full time? Or, on a domestic stage, how about Manchester City's two injury-time goals against QPR, on the last day of the season in 2012, to snatch their first Premiership title in half a century?

Certainly, it's not all about numbers, and turning round a three-goal deficit is not exceptional. In recent years Sweden (against Germany) and Newcastle United (against Arsenal) have come back from 4-0 to snatch a point. On 18 September 1976 Bayern Munich proved you can not only come back from four goals down with 35 minutes to play, you can go

Liverpool players charge towards Jerzy Dudek, who has just saved Andriy Shevchenko's penalty, completing one of football's great comebacks.

on to win. Losing 4-0 at Bochum, Bayern contrived to win 6-5, with Uli Hoeness scoring his side's sixth. On 22 August 1998, Olympique de Marseille left it even later. At home to Montpellier, they went 4-0 down in 34 minutes. That scoreline stood until 61 minutes. Then Marseille scored five, including a last-minute penalty converted by Laurent Blanc, to win 5-4.

Naturally, you have to rate comebacks higher if they are pulled off against superior – or strong – opposition, or if the circumstances are against you. One of the most famous league games in Dutch history is the clash between Heerenveen and Ajax on 7 May 1950. In the 61st minute, a certain

Rinus Michels converted a penalty for Ajax to make it 5-1 for the visitors. Then Abe Lenstra, a Heerenveen legend, scored the home side's second goal and somehow the roof fell in on Ajax. Heerenveen won 6-5. Heerenveen and Lenstra specialised in that kind of comeback. In June 1947, they were 4-0 down against Masstricht's MVV after half an hour, but three minutes from time Lenstra scored the 7-6 winner – during the play-offs for the national title, no less.

In England, Charlton Athletic's comeback against Huddersfield Town on December 21 1957, in the old Second Division, is often regarded as the mother of all comebacks. In the days before substitutions, the Addicks lost their captain Derek Ufton after he dislocated his shoulder after 15 minutes and trailed 5-1 after 62 minutes. Then Johnny Summers made history by leading ten men to a stunning win. Adopting the simple credo 'We've got nothing to lose so every time I get a chance I'll have a crack,' Summers scored five that day (including a six-minute hat-trick) and set up two more for an amazing 7-6 win. His wife Betty said: 'What a weekend this has been and right on top of Christmas too.'

The Germans, too, do fine comebacks. In the 1985–86 Cup Winners' Cup quarter-finals, West Germany's Bayer Uerdingen needed to score five goals in a hurry to complete a miraculous comeback against a Dynamo Dresden side featuring Matthias Sammer, Ulf Kirsten and Torsten Gütschow. The East German side had won the first leg 2-0 and with 58 minutes of the return leg gone, led 3-1 on the night and 5-1 on aggregate. Under the away-goals rule, Uerdingen had to score five goals in 32 minutes. Inexplicably, they scored six. After the game, either out of fear or hope of a better life, Dresden winger Frank Lippmann snuck out of the team's hotel, defecting to the West.

Yet the heroics of Bayer and Charlton don't quite compare with the most amazing comeback, all things and even lower leagues considered, we have heard of. This veritable miracle took place on 10 November 2002 in Germany's multi-tiered sixth division, in Marienheide, thirty miles east of Cologne, where the local team took on Meckenheim. Marienheide scored twice in the first half and when Meckenheim's sweeper was sent off, the hosts increased their lead until it was 5-0 with only seven – yes, seven! – minutes left. (And, remember, against ten men.) But in the 83rd minute, Meckenheim scored a consolation goal. And another in the 86th minute. And another in the 88th. 'I have never seen anything like it,' Marienheide's director of football, Wolfgang Brunzel, who watched the drama with growing horror, said later. 'This was a harmless opponent! But our players must have paid more attention to the results coming in from the other grounds than to their own match.' With 60 seconds left, Meckenheim made it 5-4. And three minutes into stoppage time, they levelled the most unlikely of games at 5-5.

⚽ Who made the most consecutive league appearances?

Common sense says it has to be a goalie. Goalkeepers are not necessarily less injury-prone than outfield players, but since they don't have to be constantly in motion or don't need explosive acceleration over the first few yards, they can play even if they are carrying the kind of minor injuries that sideline team-mates. On top of that, goalkeepers are less likely to be benched and/or be suspended for accumulating bookings. And, before the rule about denying a player an obvious goalscoring opportunity was enforced, they had to work terribly hard to be sent off.

In France, the marathon man is keeper Fabien Cool, who made 306 consecutive appearances for Auxerre between 1998 and 2007. In Italy, it's the inevitable Dino Zoff, whose record tally stands at 332: 330 for Juventus between 1972 and 1983 and two at Napoli, for whom he played the final two games of 1971–72. In Argentina, Pedro Catalano stood between the sticks day in, day out, for Deportivo Español de Buenos Aires between June 1986 and November 1994 and beats Zoff by one game: 333.

Football writers and commentators use the adjective 'unbelievable' far too often, but it's appropriate here. Because unbelievably, the British record is held by the Tranmere Rovers centre-half Harold Bell, who played 401 league games in succession between 1946 and 1955. His record run was broken when he was dropped as an emergency centre-forward on 30 August 1955. Disappointed, because his run hadn't been ended by injury, the Bootle-born defender sat with his wife in the stands and watched Tranmere draw 1-1 with Gateshead.

Yet Cool, Zoff, Catalano and even Bell are all left in the shade by Bayern and West Germany keeper Sepp Maier. He was in Bayern's goal on 20 August 1966, the first match of the 1966–67 season, and he was still in goal on the final day of the season 13 years later, 9 June 1979. He thus made 442 consecutive Bundesliga appearances. That run wasn't interrupted for any of the usual reasons – injury, loss in form, suspension, a coach who didn't like him – but by a dreadful car accident that ended Maier's career. In July 1979, the keeper crashed into a stationary car in the fast lane, sustained internal injuries and hung up his gloves.

Maier had already been involved in a car crash in 1975, when he wrote off his Ferrari. But he was back in Bayern's goal for the next game. Of course he needed luck. During those 13 years, he couldn't go the distance in four matches and had to be substituted. In one of those instances, pitch invaders in Duisburg knocked him down. Yet in all four cases he was back in goal when Bayern played their next league match.

A very young Sepp Maier at the 1966 World Cup, with Franz Beckenbauer (flanked by Bernd Patzke and Friedl Lutz).

Asked to explain his extraordinary resilience, Maier said: 'I didn't miss a league game for ten years. Of course, I was lucky I didn't sustain any serious injuries, but it's also true that we weren't squeamish. What used to be a bruise is now a terrible haematoma. Back then, they gave you some cortisone and the pain was gone. In 1975, I drove my car into a ditch but I didn't see a doctor, I went to the club's Christmas party and played the next game.'

⚽ Which side were the most convincing league champions?

The best indicator of a team's superiority is not necessarily their points total or their win percentage. In some leagues, two teams are so much better than the rest that they rack up record numbers in these departments but still have a fairly close rival (Celtic and Rangers in the Scottish Premier League, Real Madrid and Barcelona in la Liga come to mind). Rather, the best way to gauge dominance is the lead a team held over second place at the end of a season. The English record stands at 18 points, set by Manchester United in 2000. Seven years later, Lyon established the French record, winning Ligue 1 by 17 points over Marseille. In Germany, Bayern won by a whopping 25-point margin in 2013 that didn't just better but pulverise the old record (which had stood at 16).

The fact that these records are all relatively recent suggests that the gap between the haves and have-nots is widening. Yet some national records come from previous eras. The Spanish record stands at 21 points and dates from 1963, when Real Madrid won the title by 12 points under the old two-points-for-a-win rule. However, using the modern three-point

Manchester United celebrate their runaway Premier League title in May 2000, having lost just three games and won twenty-eight.

system, Real's lead balloons to 21 points, because second-placed Atlético had three times as many draws.

The Italian contender also seems relatively recent. In 2007, Inter won Serie A with 97 points and led the second-placed team, Roma, by no less than 22 points. Yet it's not really a domestic record. Il Grande Torino, the magnificent Torino side that tragically perished in the Superga air disaster in 1949 were 16 points ahead of Milan when they won Serie A in 1947–48. Under today's rules, they would have won by 24 points. They also scored 125 goals, won 19 out of 20 home games and had a goal difference of +92.

Even in smaller leagues dominated by one team, it is hard to better a 24-point (Torino) or 25-point (Bayern) lead. When Rosenborg monopolised the Norwegian title in the 1990s, they never won by more than 15 points. FBK Kaunas, who all but owned the Lithuanian title for a while, only won by 21 points in 2006. In Croatia, Dinamo Zagreb won by 21 points in 2011–12, some feat given that they played only 30 games, six less than Kaunas and ten less than Il Grande Torino.

In 2011, HJK Helsinki equalled Torino's lead, winning the Veikkausliiga, Finland's top flight, 24 points ahead of Inter Turku. HJK contrived to lose four games, in a 33-match season, yet still amassed this huge lead. This puts HJK on a par, statistically speaking, with Il Grande Torino and only one point behind Bayern's all-conquering 2013 team. However, one of the world's most famous clubs can do better than all of the sides mentioned above. And easily so.

In 1972–73, Benfica won the Portuguese league 18 points ahead of Belenenses, but under the three-points-for-a-win rule, that margin would stretch to 32 points. Not bad for a season that only lasted 30 matches. Benfica won every home match, 13 away games – and drew the other two. The Eagles won their first 23 matches of the season and didn't drop a point until All Fools' Day 1973, when they were held 2-2 away at Porto, after leading 2-1 with four minutes to go. During this beautiful season, Benfica averaged 3.67 goals a game and, at the age of 31, the great Eusébio scored 40 goals to win the Golden Boot.

Yet such worthy champions were dethroned the very next season. Sporting Lisbon won the 1973–74 title, two points ahead of Benfica. The sudden fall from grace may have been sparked by a silly controversy. Jimmy Hagan, a former Sheffield United forward, coached Benfica. He was, Eusébio said, 'a strong disciplinarian ... some players were physically sick after his first training session.' A few weeks into the new season, Hagan quit after a row about the selection of players for Eusébio's testimonial between Benfica and a World XI.

If Benfica in 1972–73 were the most convincing champions, AIK must surely be the least convincing. In 1998, they won the Swedish league despite scoring just 25 goals in 26 games. Even Östers, who came last, 14th, and were relegated, managed 26. The title came down to the last day of the season. Leaders Helsingborg only had to beat relegation candidates Häcken but lost, whereas AIK won 1-0 with a goal by right-back Alexander Östlund to secure their first title in 15 years. Of the club's 26 matches, ten ended 1-1, six were 1-0 victories and three were 0-0 draws. Only twice did AIK get carried away and win 2-0.

⚽ Which is the best defensive performance in a major league?

José Mourinho's uber-efficient Chelsea shipped just 15 goals in 38 matches as they won the Premier League in 2004–05. That works out at 0.395 goals a game. Which is pretty damn good – but it's not even the best in England. In 1978–79, Liverpool won the league with a rock solid defence that shipped 16 goals in 42 games, an average of 0.381. On this occasion, the Reds come second best. If you consider only the five biggest leagues in Europe (England, France, Germany, Italy and Spain) since 1945, Cagliari were even tighter at the back when they won Serie A in 1969–70, conceding a frankly astonishing 11 goals in 30 games, 0.367 a match. They kept 20 clean sheets and only one side, Juventus, managed to score two goals against them – though the Sardinians held on for a 2-2 draw.

Enrico Albertosi – the big man at the back for Cagliari, in a later incarnation at Inter Milan.

The irony is that, even in Sardinia, this Cagliari side is best remembered for the goalscoring prowess of Luigi Riva who was Serie A's most prolific striker that season with 21 goals in 28 appearances. In the celebrations that followed the *scudetto*, several non-Cagliari fans had been forced, at gunpoint, to wear Riva shirts. Yet the title would not have been won without the agility of goalkeeper Enrico Albertosi, who kept goal for Italy in the 1966 and 1970 World Cups. 'When I first heard of Cagliari's interest, I didn't want to go because in Florence we'd always joked that Sardinia was a penal colony,' the keeper said once. And more philsophically: 'God forbid that a goalkeeper gets devoured by doubt. A goalkeeper is never wrong, the blame is always of others.'

Oddly enough, if you widen the search a bit, you discover that, in that very season, Fenerbahçe were even more efficient than Cagliari, conceding just six goals in 30 games, 0.20 a match. That came in very handy because it meant the Istanbul side could still win their sixth league title by a seven-point margin even though their attack had scored a distinctly meagre 31 goals, a club record low.

⚽ What was the most entertaining league season ever?

There are many subjective ways of deciding how thrilling a particular season is but there are quantifiable grounds for selecting 1950 in Colombia. As David Goldblatt notes in his extraordinary book, *The Ball Is Round*, 'The League was so open and attacking that there were only six goalless draws in a whole year.' Those six came in 240 games, which included a 6-6 draw between Huracán and America de Cali, while the erstwhile Once Deportivo twice drew 5-5 (against Universidas and away at Pereira). The goals-per-game figure that season was a phenomenal 4.19.

That might have been higher if the runners-up, Millonarios, had been more ruthless. Their great player Alfredo di Stéfano, who scored 90 goals in 101 games for the club, said: 'We only scored five goals per game so as not to demoralise our opponents.' When the result was no longer in doubt, the team would switch to a passing game that became known as *Ballet Azul* (the ballet in blue – the colour of Millonarios's strip). So a team graced by the talents of Di Stéfano and his idol Adolfo Pedernera scored only 68 goals in 30 games, while Deportes Caldas, the champions, scored 91.

Credit where credit's due, this extraordinary season would never have happened without FIFA. The stampede to professionalise the Colombian game (fuelled by booming revenues from the country's staple export, coffee) meant that not all the niceties had been observed. When the amateur FA, Adefutbol, complained to FIFA, the rulers of the game decided to ban Colombian clubs and the Colombian national team. In so doing, FIFA effectively freed them from having to comply with their transfer regulations. With many Argentinian players incensed by the strikes that were paralysing football in their country, clubs like Millonarios stepped in, offering lavish salaries because there was no transfer fee to pay. When Pedernera, the heart of the legendary River Plate attack known as *La Máquina* (Machine), joined Millonarios, the revenue earned by selling tickets to his unveiling, attended by 5,000 people, was five times the typical gate receipts for a match.

Millonarios's rivals soon followed suit. By the time the 1950 season kicked off, there were 109 foreign players in Colombia (57 of them Argentinian). Among other notables were Charlie Mitten (signed from Matt Busby's Manchester United), Héctor Rial (later to win the European Cup at Real Madrid, alongside Di Stéfano), Julio Cozzi (known in Argentina as 'Goalkeeper of the Century') and Neil Franklin (the brilliant English centre-half who missed the World Cup to play for Independiente Santa Fe). This colourful cast was rounded out by such stars as Heleno de Freitas, considered Brazilian football's first '*craque problem*' (troubled genius), a gifted striker, ether addict and an inveterate womaniser whose conquests off the pitch were said to include Eva Perón.

The game was so wealthy that Deportivo Cali's Peruvian centre-forward Valeriano López used to roll up dollar bills to make his cigarettes. Legend has it that López, who scored 43 goals in 39 games for Cali, was the player Real Madrid owner

Football's first bad boy galactico, Heleno de Freitas.

Santiago Bernabéu originally travelled to Colombia to sign. When López refused, saying he didn't want to play so far away from his family, Bernabéu cast his eye over Di Stéfano.

As if the 1950 season hadn't been wild enough, the teams set a record on the very first weekend of the following campaign: on 28 and 29 July 1951, they scored 61 goals in nine games. No wonder that this era in Colombian football, which ended in 1955 when the league returned into FIFA's fold, was nicknamed El Dorado.

The only season that comes close to such thrills is 1938 in Argentina, the first professional league season in which the goals per game ratio was an astonishing 4.9. The edited highlights of this season include Racing becoming probably the only club to score 24 goals over three consecutive matches (beating Platense and Estudiantes 8-2 and Lanús 8-1), Independiente clinching the title with an 8-2 victory on the last day against Lanús, three 5-5 draws (compared to only four 0-0 draws), and Arsenio Erico, an Independiente striker idolised by a young River Plate fan called Alfredo di Stéfano, scoring 43 goals, at a rate of 1.34 a game. He could have scored more but with two games to go, he tried to set up his team-mates Antonio Sastre and Vicente de la Mata so they could score 43 goals and win a 2,000 peso reward from the cigarette company 43/70.

Erico had a wealth of nicknames – *Mister Gol*, *El Malabrista* (The Juggler), *El Hombre de Goma* (Man of Rubber), *El Diablo Sakltarín* (Jumping Devil) and *El Hombre de Mimbre* (the Wicker Man, because he scared defences and wore red) – and would be much better known if he had played for a national side. He was too loyal to his Paraguayan homeland to accept a lucrative offer to acquire Argentinian citizenship. Di Stéfano said once that Erico was better than Pelé.

PARAGUAY 2009

"EL MALABARISTA"

₲ 700

Arsenio Erico

Dirección General del Tesoro Público - Valores Fiscales

Which was the first team to win an FA Cup without English players?

Cardiff City may be the only team from outside England to win the FA Cup but their giant-killing 1-0 victory over Arsenal in 1927 was achieved with the help of gifted, English left-half Billy Hardy who was born in Bedlington, in Tyne and Wear. Known as the idol of South Wales – one report says that his mere appearance on newsreel provoked ten minutes of applause in one Cardiff cinema – Hardy was ignored by the England selectors because he played for a Welsh club.

There were three Welshmen in that Bluebirds side: skipper Fred Keenor, outside-left Ernie Curtis and forward Len Davies. In 1986, there was only one Welsh player – Ian Rush – in the Liverpool side that won what is known as the Merseyside final. Alongside Rush were four Scots (Steve Nicol, Alan Hansen, Kenny Dalglish and Kevin MacDonald), three Irishmen (Mark Lawrenson, Jim Beglin and Ronnie Whelan), one Aussie (Craig Johnston), a Dane (Jan Mølby) and a Zimbabwean (Bruce Grobbelaar). The only English player to have a small role in Liverpool's triumph was Steve McMahon who watched from the bench.

To round off this answer, it seems only appropriate to list the last all-English team to win the FA Cup: Mervyn Day, John McDowell, Frank Lampard Sr., Billy Bonds, Tommy Taylor, Kevin Lock, Billy Jennings, Graham Paddon, Alan Taylor, Trevor Brooking and Pat Holland. Under West Ham United manager John Lyall, this eleven won the 'Cockney Cup Final' of 1975, beating Fulham 2-0. The Cottagers played with ten Englishmen, including Hammers legend Bobby Moore. The only non-Englishman on the pitch that day was Fulham's Irish midfielder Jimmy Conway.

Who scored the fastest ever goal?

Brian Clough was being a bit over-optimistic when he said, 'It only takes a second to score a goal'. But in October 2011, 35-year-old Russian midfielder Mikhail Osinov found the net for MITOS Novocherkassk after just 2.68 seconds in a Russian Second Division South match. After his team-mates had kicked off and rolled the ball back, Osinov stepped forward, chipped the Olimpia Gelendzhik keeper from 51 yards and scored what could be the world's fastest ever goal.

Nawaf Al-Abed would dispute that. In November 2009, the Saudi striker scored after just two seconds – with an improbable shot from the halfway line that caught the keeper out of position – for Al Hilal against Al Shoalah in a Prince Faisal bin Fahad Cup match. Unfortunately for Al-Abed, this was an Under-23 tournament and the game was ruled invalid after some killjoy spotted that Al Hilal used six over-age players in the second half.

So Osinov is still, for now, the fastest scorer in the professional game. But fans of the Isle of Wight's Cowes Sports FC will tell you that their striker Marc Burrows was even quicker off the mark. In 2004, assisted by a strong wind, Burrows scored for Cowes Reserves after 2.5 seconds against Eastleigh Reserves. He was modest enough to admit: 'I've tried something similar once or twice but the ball normally goes out for a throw in making me feel a right prat.' The FA declared: 'This is the fastest goal we are aware of' which seemed to implicitly acknowledge that at this level of the game, it's possible that many such goals are scored and simply not timed.

One of the difficulties in making a definitive call is that, as Ray Spiller of the Association of Football Statisticians has pointed out, there is no system for officially recognising the timing of goals. So, for example, when Jim Fryatt scored for Bradford Park Avenue against Tranmere in 1964, referee Bob Simons still had his stopwatch in hand after blowing the whistle and timed the strike at four seconds. There is no film evidence to contradict him. The fastest goal in a national competition is probably Colin Cowperthwaite's strike after 3.56 seconds for Barrow against Kettering Town in the Alliance Premier League on 8 December 1979.

Torquay United defender Pat Kruse has the unfortunate distinction of scoring the fastest own goal in British history, heading past his own keeper after six seconds against Cambridge United in January 1977. The good news for Kruse is that his world record was broken in September 2009 when Estonian defender Jaanis Kriska took just five seconds to head into his own net in a game his side, Kuressaare, lost 8-0 to Levadia Tallinn.

The record for the fastest hat-trick belongs to Ross County striker Tommy Ross who scored three in 90 seconds against Nairn County on 28 November 1964. Because there were no timekeepers at the match, his feat was not recognised by the *Guinness Book Of Records* until 2004, after the referee had confirmed the feat. Asked how he scored so many goals in such rapid succession, Ross said: 'In those days there was no kissing and cuddling when you scored a goal. You just ran back to the halfway line and got on with the game. If you were lucky, you got a pat on the head from the captain.'

⚽ When did teams first agree to fix a match?

West Germany's 1-0 victory over Austria in Spain in the 1982 World Cup is the most infamous example of this nefarious practice. With the other teams in Group 2, Algeria and Chile, playing their last match the day before, Germany and

Austria knew this result would take them both through to the second round. Algeria, who had four points, were denied the chance to make history as the first African nation to quality for the second stage of a World Cup.

There is no credible evidence of a pre-match conspiracy to fix the result so this was, if you will, a spontaneous fix. After ten minutes, Horst Hrubesch scored for West Germany. Three minutes later, Wolfgang Dremmler went clear through and was one-on-one with the keeper. If he had made it 2-0, Austria would have been forced to attack. After that, both sides saw little point in taking the risk of going forward, so there were no crosses or shots on goal. Algerian supporters in the crowd started waving banknotes at the players in outrage. As play wore on – and the denouement became painfully obvious – German commentator Eberhard Stanjek was almost sobbing as he complained: 'What is happening here is disgraceful and has nothing to do with football.' FIFA let the result stand – but changed the rules so that the last round of games in a group would always be played at the same time.

The German and Austrian teams and associations initially seemed baffled by the outrage. Hans Tschak, the head of the Austrian delegation, said: 'Naturally today's game was played tactically. But if 10,000 "Sons of the Desert" here in the stadium want to trigger a scandal because of this it just goes to show that they have too few schools. Some sheikh comes out of an oasis, is allowed to get a sniff of World Cup air after 300 years and thinks he's entitled to open his gob.'

The outrage, from everyone else, was so universal, it is easy to assume that such an arrangement was unprecedented. Yet, as Joe McGinniss has suggested in his delightful book *The Miracle Of Castel Di Sangro*, such arrangements were not uncommon in Italian football. In 1979, in the last round of Serie A matches, relegation-threatened Avellino were losing 3-0 away to third-

Softly, softly. The West Germans match the Austrians in the World Cup's disgraceful 1982 'phoney war'.

placed Juventus. Then the *Bianconeri*'s talismanic keeper Dino Zoff was replaced, with 20 minutes to go, by an unknown youngster called Giancarlo Andresselli. Avellino scored three goals to make it 3-3 and earn the draw that left them in 10th place with 26 points, two points above the relegation zone.

Six years earlier, in 1973, concern about an outbreak of dubious draws in the USSR's First Division prompted the Soviets to introduce a novelty we associate with the capitalist North American leagues: penalty shoot-outs to decide drawn games. (The team that won the shoot-out were given the point for the draw, the loser got nothing: Kairat Alma-Ata set some kind of record by drawing 11 games and winning ten of those shoot-outs.)

Non-aggression pacts, of the Germany–Austria variety, are probably as old as the game itself. When the English Football

League started, relegation and promotion was initially decided by an end of season mini-league between the two bottom teams in the First Division and the two top teams in the Second Division. In April 1898, the four teams involved in what were then called test matches were Blackburn Rovers, Burnley, Newcastle United and Stoke City. Before Burnley and Stoke kicked off their final game they knew – just as precisely as the teams in Gijón – which scoreline would suit them both. A draw would ensure Burnley and Stoke were in the top division. Neither team took any chances – or made any – in a draw that went down in history as the match without a shot. The 4,000 supporters at Stoke's Victoria Ground were so disgusted they tried to stop the game by keeping the ball whenever it strayed into the stands and even kicked one ball into the river Trent. The appalled Football League extended the First Division to 18 teams to include Newcastle and Blackburn.

In goal for Burnley, with nothing to do in that farcical fixture, was the controversial figure of 'Happy Jack' Hillman, one of the most likely instigators of the non-aggression pact with Stoke. Good enough to win a cap for England, Hillman had returned to the Clarets after being fined by Dundee for 'not trying' during matches. Ten months after the deadlock at Stoke, justice was done. Burnley were relegated after losing their last game 4-0 to Nottingham Forest, whose skipper Archie Macpherson claimed Hillman had offered his players £2 a head (£150 in today's money) to 'take it easy'. The 27-year-old keeper insisted he was only joking but the FA banned him for 12 months. The English game's first match-fixer, Hillman never played for his country again.

⚽ Which team has won the most games on the trot?

In 2010–11, Pep Guardiola's all-conquering Barcelona won 16 games in a row in la Liga, a record in Spain but not in Europe, as Benfica supporters were quick to point out: the Eagles had racked up 29 successive victories between 1971 and 1973. But Al-Faisaly, serial winners from Amman, can top that. Jordan's greatest club side won 32 matches on the trot between August 2001 and March 2003 as they monopolised the Jordanian title.

As a point of comparison, the longest winning streak in English league football is 14, a record shared by Arsenal (spanning the end of 2001–02 and the start of 2002–03 in the Premier League), Bristol City (Division Two, 1905–06), Manchester United (Division Two, 1904–05), and Preston North End (Division Two, 1950–51). Martin O'Neill's Celtic, who won 25 in a row in 2003–04, hold the British club record.

The impressive runs by Al-Faisaly, Arsenal, Barcelona, Benfica and Celtic are not record-breaking. Not by a long way. Between 1919 and 1924, Sparta Prague won an astonishing 54 games in a row in the Czechoslovakian League (including three wins in an end of season mini-tournament in 1919 and one victory in a national play-off in 1922). In 1923, the most lustrous season in this golden era, Sparta scored 94 goals as they won all 15 matches to clinch their fifth title in a row.

No one has yet been proven to have beaten Sparta's record. Their tally may be even greater than 54: it is not clear, given the sketchy state of Czech football statistics from this era, at exactly what point during the 1924 season Iron Sparta astounded themselves, their supporters and their rivals by drawing or losing a game.

The Iron Sparta team of 1922, with Scottish coach John Dick in his tweed suit. Alas, the keeper here is not the comedian Vlasta Burian.

This invincible outfit were inevitably known as Iron Sparta. The photograph of the 1922 team on the club website describes the team as 'almost unbeatable' and shows the team's Scottish manager, a former Arsenal centre-half called John Dick, in suit, hat and tie giving the photographer his best 'can we get this over with?' stare. Iron Sparta's relentless efficiency was especially impressive given that their goalkeeper Vlasta Burian was hardly the embodiment of single-minded professional focus. A cabaret artist, comedian and manic depressive, Burian starred in his first movie in 1923, becoming so successful he was dubbed the king of Czech comedy, had a rose named after him and considered running for president.

🌑 Which team has endured the worst goalscoring drought?

'**I would wait 500 minutes** and I would wait 500 more, just to be the man who waits a thousand minutes to see our wee country score.' The modified Proclaimers anthem, *500 Miles,* was a constant solace to Northern Ireland fans who watched their team play a record 1,298 minutes – that's thirteen-and-a-half games over a period of two years and five days – without finding the back of the net once.

The drought began after David Healy scored the only goal for Northern Ireland against Malta in a World Cup qualifier on 6 October 2001. The barren streak cost manager Sammy McIlroy his job before it was ended – by Healy – in the 56th minute of a 4-1 defeat at Windsor Park against Norway on 18 February 2004. Healy, Northern Ireland's all-time top scorer, said afterwards: 'It was good to get that monkey off our back.'

Such suffering would not impress Stirling Albion fans who, in 1981, watched their beloved Binos get relegated from the Scottish First Division after scoring their last goal of the season in a 1-0 win against Dunfermline on 31 January. Not even extra penalty-taking sessions could end this dismal run. The most remarkable aspect of this debacle is that manager Alex Smith, who had won the Division Two title with the club in 1977, kept his job.

Albion finally broke their duck after 14 matches and 1,292 minutes on 8 August 1981 in a 4-1 loss to Falkirk, though the turnaround in the club's fortunes was far from instant: in October 1981, the Binos' away support had fallen to six. But on 8 December 1984, Stirling recorded the biggest win in the senior game in Britain in the twentieth century, beating Selkirk 20-0 in the Scottish Cup. Smith was still in the dugout then and admitted later: 'I must have lost count, I thought it was 19-0.' He may just have been flabbergasted that Albion could score 20 in one match when they had managed only 18 in their entire First Division season in 1980–81.

⚽ Which player has had the longest goalscoring streak?

If we're talking sheer quantities of goals, Middlesbrough centre-forward George Camsell's streak takes some beating. Between 16 October 1926 and 1 January 1927, 'the pitman turned poacher supreme', in the words of the *Middlesbrough Evening Gazette*, was never off the scoresheet, scoring 29 goals in 12 games. In that astonishing run, he scored all five goals as Boro beat Manchester City 5-3 away from home on Christmas Day, four against Portsmouth, Fulham and Swansea City, and a hat-trick against Port Vale. He finally failed to get his name on the scoresheet in a 0-0 draw against Chelsea on 15 January.

SUN SOCCERCARD No 223

G. CAMSELL (England)

To be fair to Camsell, it is worth pointing out that his run really extended to 13 games in a row because he scored in a 5-3 win against Leicester City in the FA Cup on 8 January but the inclusion of a domestic cup match, football statistics from across the globe being as inconsistent as they are, would make it virtually impossible to compare like with like. That season, Camsell set a Football League record with 59 goals in a season, a feat that would be better remembered today if a young hotshot called Dixie Dean hadn't scored 60 for Everton the very next season.

Camsell is doubly unlucky because, in the very season he was scoring for fun – for once, the cliché seems appropriate – Wolves forward Tom Phillipson scored 22 goals in a 13-game scoring streak. (This is still a Football League record.)

You may wonder why so many scorers were in such prolific form in this era. Apart from the considerable talents of the strikers concerned, there was the small matter of the new offside law. From 1925, there only needed to be two players between the attacker and the goal when the ball was played. The statistics show just how demoralising this change was for defenders. In 1924–25, 4,700 goals were scored in 1,848 Football League matches. In 1925–26, that figure was 6,373.

Still, some strikers have kept their goalscoring runs going without a change in the law. Phillipson's record is equalled by Peter Dubovsky's 13-match run for his home town side Slovak Bratislava in 1991–92. (Mind you, eight of his 18 goals in that streak were penalties.) The club won the title and Dubovsky joined Real Madrid where he lost the battle for a first-team place with a young Raúl. Still revered as a genius in Slovakia, Dubosvky rebuilt his career at Oviedo but in June 2000, he fell to his death taking pictures of a waterfall in the Thai resort of Ko Samui. He was just 28.

Three players are on record as having a 15-game scoring streak: Tor Henning Hamre (Flora Tallinn, 2003, 21 goals including four penalties); Jaime Riveros (Santiago Wanderers, 2004, 21 goals, including seven penalties) and Juan Pedro Young (Penarol, 1933, 22 goals, no penalties). Pelé has claimed to have been on the scoresheet in 14 or 16 games in a row for Santos, but the precise details are hard to pin down.

Two players who are recorded to have scored in 16 league games are Teodor Peterek and the inevitable Gerd Müller.

Peterek scored 22 goals (including five penalties) in 16 matches for Ruch Chorzow in 1937 and 1938 (his run spanned two seasons). Alongside Gerard Wodarz and Ernst Willimowski, Peterek formed one of the greatest attacking tridents the Polish game has ever seen. They were at their peak when World War II effectively ended their careers. After playing for Bismarckhütter SV, the Nazified version of Ruch Chorzow, Peterek was conscripted into the Wehrmacht, escaping to join the Allies. After the war, he returned to Chorzow and played a few games for his old club. But he was 39 by then and soon hung up his boots for good.

Müller's streak dates from 1969–70. Stattos sometimes overlook it, because inclement weather played havoc with a few matchdays and there were Bayern games that had to be postponed by almost three months, a fact that only shows up in record books which ignore the sequence of the matchdays but list the games chronologically. The run started on 27 September 1969 with a goal against Braunschweig (Brunswick) and ended on 3 March

1970 with a goal against Frankfurt. In those 16 games, Müller scored 23 goals. Two of them came from the penalty spot, something we only bring up because it allows us to mention that Müller holds the Bundesliga record for penalties missed. (He took 63 and missed 12.)

Müller's streak ended on 7 March in the Munich derby and on a tricky, snowy surface. The Bomber had only two chances to score and wasted both. For the remainder of the game, the Yugoslav Željko Perušić marked him closely.

So, 16 was the record – set 75 years ago, tied 43 years ago but broken, just last season, by Lionel Messi . On 11 November 2012, matchday 11 in the Primera División season, he scored twice against Mallorca. He also did this, scoring a brace, on the next five – yes, five – matchdays. He lost momentum and scored only one goal per match in four games on the trot. Then he closed in on Camsell's territory, finding the net four times against Osasuna. And on and on it went. Until 9 March 2013. Messi had therefore scored in 16 consecutive league games, tying with Peterek and Müller (and obliterating the old Spanish record, which had stood at 10 games).

But when Barcelona hosted Deportivo La Coruña on 9 March 2013, Messi sat on the bench for more than an hour before finally coming on. With 130 seconds left on the clock, he dribbled past three defenders, played the ball to Dani Alves and ran into the box. He received Alves's pass seven yards in front of goal and with the keeper

moving in on him. There was no time to trap the ball and no space to hit it into. So Messi simply chipped the ball over the goalkeeper and into the net with his first touch. If ever a goal was worthy of setting a new world record, this was it.

Three weeks later, on 30 March 2013, Messi was on target against Celta Vigo to score in Barcelona's 19th consecutive game. He'd scored 30 goals during that run (among them three penalties). Messi then missed Barça's next three league encounters. Upon his return, against Bilbao, he scored nine minutes after coming on deep into the second half. Eight days later, he scored two goals aginst Real Betis to make it 21 in a row. And then, on the final day of the season, he played 90 minutes away at Atlético Madrid – but failed to hit the net.

Does **home advantage** really exist?

In 2005, reviewing a biography of José Mourinho in the *London Review of Books*, David Runciman wrote: 'The clearest evidence that mysterious forces are at work on the sports field comes from the unarguable impact of home advantage in almost every kind of sporting contest. There has been a lot of academic work on this phenomenon, but there is nowhere near as much consensus about what is causing it.'

Part of the problem is that the factors which used to account for home advantage – the fatigue of away journeys, discomfort of hotel beds, unfamiliarity with the playing surface, the intimidating power of signs like 'This is Anfield' – have been greatly reduced. As Runciman wrote: 'These days, no big league team should ever arrive at an away game tired, tetchy, homesick (the top players lead such bicoastal, transcontinental, post-nuclear lives that it's not clear what it would mean for them to be homesick anyway); yet winning away from home is still very hard.'

The famous 'This is Anfield' sign. It didn't quite work for Roy Hodgson.

His explanation was twofold. 'Familiarity with one's surroundings, however anonymous they might appear from the outside, seems to enhance confidence in the performance of repetitive physical tasks.' Other studies have suggested that testosterone levels, an important predictor of victory in many sports, rise among players defending their own patch. 'The other thing that improves performance is an audience,' says Runciman. He isn't referring to the vaunted power of certain sections of grounds – notably the Stretford End or the Kop – to inspire their players, influence referees and, as the cliché suggests, suck the ball into goal. For Runciman, the important factor isn't how much noise home fans make – the prawn sandwich scoffers at Old Trafford are often out-sung by the away crowd – but their sheer, reassuring presence. Research has also consistently shown that officials are unwittingly influenced by home crowds.

Such challenges may sound insurmountable. Yet away teams are having increasing success surmounting them. In 2008, Dortmund University published a study which said that until 1987–88, home teams won 55.8 percent of their games. But gradually they began scoring less – while conceding the same number of goals – on their own turf. So between 1987–88 and 2006–07, the home side only won 47.8 percent of games. That trend has continued since. Let's be clear, home sides are still more likely to grab three points than their visitors (who only won 27.1 percent of the time in the top flights in England, Germany, Italy, the Netherlands and Spain in 2011–12, according to Betfair's statistics) but that advantage has been significantly eroded. Typically today, a side in one of those leagues will win around 47.6 percent of their home games.

One unpublished study of home advantage in football in la Liga since it was founded in 1928 has suggested that this factor is important to some clubs but not for others. Only nine teams have won the Spanish title and seven of them – Athletic Bilbao, Atlético Madrid, Deportivo la Coruña, Real Betis, Real Sociedad, Sevilla and Valencia – counted on home advantage. The other two – Barcelona (who have 21 titles) and Real Madrid (32) – don't distinguish between the two types of fixture. They expect to win every match.

In 2010–11, when Pep Guardiola's *Blaugranas* broke records on their way to the title, they won their first ten games away from home and became the first team in the history of la Liga to score in every away game. The difference between their home and away form came down, in essence, to the fact that they drew three more games on the road than they did at Camp Nou.

What is the **longest move that has led to a goal?**

'**It was only when** there was absolutely nobody left you could pass the ball to that we finally put it into the net.' In these days of tiki-taka, the patient short-passing game perfected by the Spanish, you'd probably expect a Barcelona player to have uttered these words not so long ago. Yet they are more than half a century old and come from a German defender by the name of Hans Bornemann, who was describing the style his club, Schalke 04, made famous when he was a player in the 1930s. So the idea of stringing many passes together to create an opening is pretty old. Yet goals from very long moves do seem to be a product of the very modern era, in which ball possession is so prized. At least every impressive example is of fairly recent origin.

True, there is Carlos Alberto's great goal that capped Brazil's 4-1 win in the 1970 World Cup final, in which eight outfield players touched the ball before their captain fired home. It is often cited as a near-perfect example of a goal that puts the finishing touch on an extended move. But there were only nine passes in this 29-second move – and a bit of virtuoso dribbling from defender Clodoaldo to befuddle three Italians. This is nowhere near what you have to come up with to be in the running for a really, really long move.

Such as the arguably most magical 58 seconds of the 2006 World Cup. The move that led to Argentina's second goal in their 6-0 rout of Serbia and Montenegro involved nine players and ended with a back-heeler from Hernán Crespo to set up the eventual scorer Esteban Cambiasso. An American statistician by the name of David R. Brillinger published a 20-page academic paper on this goal, entitled *A Potential*

Carlos Alberto celebrates his classic goal in the 1970 World Cup Final, following pass number nine from Pelé.

Function Approach to the Flow of Play in Soccer. Brillinger does many strange things in his paper – such as expounding on 'the potential function of Newtonian gravity' – but he does state correctly that the number of passes was 25. There is some disagreement about this, as many sources say there were 24. The controversy seems to surround the very first pass, as Maxi Rodriguez robbed an opponent in possession by poking the ball towards his own defence. Yet he intentionally played the ball to Gabriel Heinze, which means that this was the first pass and Crespo's back-heeler the 25th.

In any case, the exact number of passes doesn't make that much difference, as there have been longer moves. As you might expect, Barcelona have scored after stringing together more passes – 27 – in fewer seconds – 33 – than Argentina. The move that led to this goal at Anfield in 2001 started with a throw-in (which doesn't count as a pass) and ended when Xavi, after a seemingly endless succession of short passes, beat the offside trap with a 30-yard through-ball setting up Marc Overmars to round the goalkeeper and slot home.

Yet even this awe-inspiring display of tiki-taka pales into insignificance compared to a 35-pass move that led to a goal in April 2006. This work of art was created by Fenerbahçe in a combustible Istanbul derby with Galatasaray. Leading 3-0 after 78 minutes, Fener won the ball at the edge of their area. In the next 88 seconds, the team passed the ball around 34 times until Ümit Özat got behind the defence on the left wing. He crossed into the box – pass number 35 – for Nicolas Anelka to score with a first-time shot and make it 4-0. The move involved every outfield player and there were only three moments during the move when an opponent was close enough to the ball to have a reasonable chance of intercepting a pass.

⚽ Who took the first penalty?

This is surprisingly hard to answer with any certainty. Many reference books and websites confidently cite names and dates. For example, until recent weeks Wikipedia simply stated: 'The first ever penalty kick was awarded to Wolverhampton Wanderers in their game against Accrington at Molineux Stadium on 14 September 1891. The penalty was taken and scored by Billy Heath as Wolves went on to win the game 5–0.' There was even a footnote that told you the source of this information, the BBC.

Yet when you looked up the BBC website in question ('Funny Old Game – Happened On This Day'), you realised that Wikipedia had left out a vital four words, because the text says that on this date in history 'Wolverhampton Wanderers' John Heath converts the first penalty kick in the Football League in a game against Accrington Stanley'. The words that make all the difference here are, of course, 'in the Football League'. Clark Miller's history of the spot-kick, *He Always Puts It to the Right*, says a player by the name of Farman converted one on 5 September 1891 for Newton Heath against Blackpool in the Lancashire League. Miller doesn't say Farman was the first, merely the first 'in England'.

The International Football Association Board introduced the penalty kick during a meeting at the Alexandra Hotel in Glasgow (bear that in mind) on 2 June 1891, some four months after a scandalous match between Stoke and Notts County in which County defender John Hendry deliberately handled the ball on the goal-line to prevent the equaliser. The man who proposed a new, harsh penalty to become effective the following season (bear that in mind, too) for such unsportsmanlike conduct was, ironically, a goalkeeper – William McCrum, who played for Irish side Milford.

Obviously, there was plenty of time between 2 June and Farman's goal on 5 September to take penalties somewhere on the British Isles. A German book on the history of the spot-kick – *Elfmeter!* by René Martens – credits one J. Dalton as the pioneer. It is a tantalising claim because this player happened to be Canadian, in a select XI touring Ireland. On 29 August 1891, they played Linfield at Ulsterville. As George Glass, the leading Belfast statistician, writes: 'During the match Willie Gordon, the Linfield right back handled the ball in the penalty box. Dalton the Canadian right half took the penalty and scored. This was the first penalty kick taken on Irish soil.'

That John Terry moment in Moscow. The golden rule, when taking the vital penalty in a Champions League final, is not to slip as you kick the ball.

But we have more candidates – and one more country: Scotland. The blog *Association Football Before the 'D'* (meaning the half-circle at the edge of the penalty area that was introduced in 1937) says: 'The first goal from a penalty kick was scored by Alex McCall for Renton FC against Leith Athletic on August 22nd 1891.'

And there is talk of an even earlier penalty. A 2009 discussion on *Scottishleague.net* unearthed a match between Airdrieonians and Royal Albert on 6 June 1891, during which 'the referee awarded [a penalty kick] by mistake because although the penalty rule had been passed three days earlier it wasn't due to become law until [the new season]'. The game in question was the Airdrie Charity Cup final played at Mavisbank and the Airdrieonian who put the penalty away was called McLuggage.

⚽ What match has prompted the most red cards?

In October 2012, officials in a junior league match in Paraguay issued 36 red cards after the game between Teniente Farina and Libertad ended in a mass brawl. The trigger for the melee was referee Nestor Guillen's decision to send off two players in the closing minutes. They refused to leave the pitch, continuing to feud until their team-mates joined in. Appalled by the melee, flying kicks and punches, Guillen and his assistants left the pitch and, even though they were in the dressing room when the violence peaked, issued 36 red cards, dismissing every player on the field and on the bench.

You would think that would be a record. It is, but only a joint one. Exactly the same number were issued in March 2011 by Argentinian referee Damian Rubino after a match in the fifth tier between Claypole and Victoriano Arenas finished in much the same violent fashion. The only difference being that fans and coaches joined in this brawl.

As bad, mad and undisciplined as that sounds, it could have been far worse. In February 2010, Hawick United striker Paul Cooper was banned for two years by the Scottish FA after being shown two yellow cards – and five reds – in a Borders League Amateur Match. Cooper was so incensed by his second booking he subjected referee Andy Lyon to a stream of verbal abuse as he left the pitch and persisted even as the red cards mounted. The 39-year-old, nicknamed Santa by his team-mates, did apologise to the official later, admitting: 'I overreacted.'

Red and yellow cards, incidentally, have a very recent history. In the old days, refereees 'put players in their book' and pointed to the touchline for a dismissal. But in the 1966

World Cup things got confusing during the charged game between England and Argentina, when both Charltons were reported as being booked (the ref wasn't too clear about this) and Argentina's Rattin was sent off. English referee Ken Aston suggested that red and yellow cards, based on internationaly recognised traffic light colours, could help matters, and they were duly introduced at the 1970 Mexico World Cup.

Which is the greatest relegation escape act of all-time?

Long before 'the great escape' had become a movie, and a cliché of relegation battles, Lincoln City had shredded their supporters' nerves with a survival story that defied belief. With six matches left in the Second Division in 1957–58, the Imps were five points from safety (in an era when a victory was worth two points), had not won in their last 18 matches and had with dismal consistency just lost nine in a row.

Yet six games – and six victories – later, the Imps survived the drop by one point, at Notts County's expense. The tide turned with Lincoln's 3-1 win away to Barnsley on 8 April. The result was even more astonishing because, only the day before, in their Easter Monday fixture, they had lost at home to the Tykes by the same scoreline. During that defeat, one despondent Lincoln fan scaled the Sincil Bank flagpole to lower the club's colours to half mast. Yet the players were made of sterner stuff. With journeyman striker Ron Harbertson, a late signing from Darlington, scoring nine goals in 11 games, the Imps survived. Their Roy Of The Rovers-style comeback came to a fitting end when Harbertson scored the relegation-averting goal with a 30-yard shot that was so hard it broke the stanchion.

For all of Lincoln's heroics, the world's greatest escapologist, the Hungarian-born American Harry Houdini, would probably prefer the great escape staged by SC Freiburg in 1994. A magician who liked to create a fantastic, mysterious aura around his shows, Houdini would have been thrilled to hear that the German club's survival that year was partly inspired by a phantom goal.

With three games left in the Bundesliga in 1993–94, Freiburg trailed 15th-placed Nuremberg by four points and one goal. After four months without a single league victory, Freiburg went on to win their last three games, two of which were away from home. Under the old two-points-for-a-win rule, this meant that Nuremberg needed one win and one draw from three games to stay up. They got a win (a commanding 4-1 against Wattenscheid) and were drawing the Bavarian derby with Bayern Munich when this happened ...

A corner from the right was flicked on towards the far post of Nuremberg's goal, where Bayern's Thomas Helmer bundled the ball into touch from two yards out. While Nuremberg's keeper Andreas Köpke patted Helmer on the back to console him for missing such a sitter, the linesman raised his flag to signal a goal. Despite fierce protests – and even though the ball rolled many yards into touch – the referee trusted his assistant and gave Bayern the goal.

Nuremberg lost the game 2-1 after missing a late penalty but quickly filed a protest and the German FA annulled the game. The decision infuriated FIFA, which strictly opposed this kind of 'trial by television', but German officials argued that what had already become notorious as the Phantom Goal constituted such a blatant error that the rules of fair play demanded Nuremberg were given another chance. They were. They lost the replay 5-0 and went down on goal difference. Sadly, it was not a phantom goal difference.

⚽ What is the lowest number of penalties a team has scored in a shoot-out and still won?

None. That's right – Rangers missed all four spot kicks in the shoot-out against Sporting Lisbon in the second round of the Cup Winners' Cup on 3 November 1971 yet still progressed. The incident has become part of the club's folklore but for non-Gers fans, let's explain how it happened.

Rangers won the first leg at Ibrox 3-2 and, after 90 minutes of the second leg in Lisbon, were behind by the same scoreline. In extra time, both sides found the net so the match finished 4-3 to Sporting. With the sides still level on aggregate, Dutch referee Laurens van Ravens ordered a penalty shoot-out which Sporting won. The Rangers players trudged back to the dressing room in dejection. Rangers star Willie Henderson recalled later: 'There was something in my head about away goals but it seemed we were out.' Indeed, even as the kicks were being taken, Rangers manager Willie Waddell was pointing out to UEFA delegate Andre Ramirez that the shoot-out should never have taken place, that Rangers – having scored three away goals to Sporting's two – were in the third round and that the referee was breaking the rules.

Van Ravens' mistake, it should be noted, was not as inexplicable as it would be today. Until 1970, the away goals rule (created in 1965) only applied to goals scored during regular time. Still, when Van Ravens blundered, the new version of the rule had been in effect for well over a season. As he later recalled: 'After the penalties, I returned to the dressing room. There the UEFA officials told me the good news and the bad news. The good news was that I had controlled an excellent game well. The bad news – Rangers should have won the match.'

With the proper away goals rule enforced, Rangers won the tie. Six months later, in Barcelona, they beat Dynamo Moscow 3-2 to win the Cup Winners Cup. That team are fondly recalled as the Barcelona Bears. Yet even this triumph was not without controversy. Rangers were denied the chance of defending the trophy when hundreds of their fans invaded the pitch. As a riot raged, the trophy was presented to Waddell and skipper John Greig in an office deep beneath the Camp Nou stands. UEFA called the Scottish fans' behaviour 'shocking and ugly' and banned the club from European competition for a year.

⚽ Has any single club supplied an entire international team?

In the very first international, a 0-0 draw between England and Scotland on 30 November 1872, Queen's Park supplied all 11 Scottish players. The Scottish selectors had hoped that Royal Engineers striker Henry Renny-Tailyour and the Wanderers star Arthur Kinnaird would turn out for them but both were unavailable so they turned to their leading club to field the whole team. As there was no Scottish League then, the Scottish Cup and the Scottish FA weren't founded until 1873, and neither Rangers or Celtic had been properly established, the selectors may have felt they had little option.

On 30 September 1964, modern football history was made at half-time in a match between Belgium and the Netherlands in Antwerp when Guy Delhasse was replaced in the home side's goal by Jean Trappeniers. After that switch, Belgium played the rest of the match with a national side drawn entirely from Anderlecht. Having 11 Mauves on the pitch

England captain Eddie Hapgood introduces his Arsenal team-mate George Male to Prince Arthur of Connaught and the Italian ambassador before the legendary Battle of Highbury.

made the Diables Rouges marginally more cohesive and Jef Jurion scored the only goal of the game in the 87th minute. Jurion was a gifted winger-turned-playmaker who played in seven positions for Belgium but is, a little unfairly, best known for always wearing spectacles on the pitch.

No club has ever supplied more than seven players in the same England team. Arsenal achieved this record in 1934, with seven players in the startling line-up in the epic, violent 3-2 win over Italy remembered in football history as the Battle of Highbury. The Gunners capped that day were keeper Frank Moss, left-back Eddie Hapgood, right-back George

Male, left half-back Wilf Copping, inside-right Ray Bowden, inside-left Cliff Bastin and centre-forward Ted Drake. Manchester United matched this record briefly on 28 March 2001 in a World Cup qualifier, though Wes Brown and Teddy Sheringham came on as subs, the latter in the 84th-minute.

Arsenal's record has never officially been challenged. The FA dismisses the persistent suggestion that Corinthians twice supplied an entire English team, in 1894 and 1895, against Wales. The problem with this theory, as the authoritative England Football Online website has pointed out, is that in both games the players credited as Corinthians also played regularly – and in some cases primarily – for other clubs too. So the Gunners' record stands in England. Seven is also the modern-era record in Germany, set by Borussia Mönchengladbach in 1971 and later equalled, inevitably, by Bayern.

There is, however, an intriguing footnote to this particular national record. After World War II, the territory known as Saarland, today one of Germany's federal states, was a protectorate and, between 1950 and 1956, a FIFA member. The Saarland national team played 19 official internationals and even took part in the 1954 World Cup qualifiers. In one of football history's great jokes, they had to face West Germany. In both games against the Germans – on 11 October 1953 and 28 March 1954 – Saarland fielded a team in which ten players came from the same club, Saarbrücken FC. The odd man out in both games was midfielder Kurt Clemens, under contract at Saarbrücken's local rivals Saar 05.

Nacional, Dynamo Kiev and Torino have all dominated their national sides to a considerable extent. In the 1970 World Cup, Uruguay fielded eight players from Nacional when they drew 0-0 with Italy in Puebla. Sixteen years later, when the Soviet Union kicked off their World Cup campaign against Hungary, the USSR coach Valeri Lobanovskiy picked eight players from Dynamo Kiev, the club he managed in his day job. In the 70th minute, when Dynamo striker Igor Belanov came off he was replaced by club team-mate Vadym Yevtushenko. Four of the goals in the USSR's 6-0 victory were scored by Dynamo players. In the last 16, against Belgium, the coach selected nine Dynamo stars in his starting eleven but despite a Belanov hat-trick, the USSR lost 4-3 in extra time to a Belgian side graced by such talents as playmaker Enzo Scifo and skipper Jan Ceulemans, who was probably five yards offside when he scored Belgium's second. Back in the USSR, few criticised Lobanovskiy's selection. Dynamo had won the Soviet league and cup in 1985 and the Cup Winners' Cup the month before the World Cup. Their dominance of the national squad was a fair reflection of their team's calibre.

The same logic prompted Vittorio Pozzo, the coach who won Italy's first two World Cups, to turn to Torino to supply all ten outfield players when the *Azzurri* faced Hungary on 11 May 1947. Goalkeeper Lucidio Sentimenti IV (so known because he was the fourth of five football-playing brothers) was the odd man out – and even he played for Turin's other team, Juventus. That Grande Torino side was the greatest team in Italian football history. They won five Serie A titles in a row, racked up enough firsts to fill their own book of records and, in April 1946, after going 6-0 up in 19 minutes away to Roma, kept their margin of victory down to 7-0 because their coach Luigi Ferrero told them there was no need to humiliate the opposition.

Against such a side, in Torino's own stadium, Hungary did well only to lose 3-2. In the 76th minute, a 22-year-old Puskás made it 2-2 with a penalty but 13 minutes later Torino midfielder Ezio Loik scored to win the match for Italy. On 9 May 1949, Loik and 17 of his Torino team-mates would die when their plane crashed into the Superga hill near Turin.

What was the longest amount of stoppage time added to a game?

In the old days, referees rarely played more than one or two minutes of stoppage time. The World Cup semi-final between France and West Germany in 1982 is a case in point. This was the game in which defender Patrick Battiston lost consciousness after being knocked down by German goalkeeper Harald Schumacher. Even though Battiston was treated on the pitch at length, Dutch referee Charles Corver added just three and a half minutes of injury time.

Yet even in the old days, the referees sometimes remembered to stop their watches. Eight years after the Battiston drama, there was another much-debated foul in another World Cup semi-final. In 1990, Italy and Argentina went into extra time at 1-1 and, for some reason, French referee Michel Vautrot added four minutes to the first period. (Some people claim he simply forgot to look at his watch.) Suddenly Italy's Roberto Baggio went down off the ball. Vautrot stopped play, consulted his Danish linesman Peter Mikkelsen and sent off Argentina's Ricardo Giusti for hitting Baggio in the face, sparking lengthy protests by Giusti's team-mates. In the ensuing melee, this first period of extra time lasted 23 minutes. One World Cup later, Scottish referee Leslie Mottram added 8 minutes and 36 seconds to a hard-fought, but largely uneventful 0-0 between South Korea and Bolivia on 24 June 1994. His reasoning remains a mystery and it can't even have been a malfunctioning watch – Mottram wore two of them.

Yet eight, nine or even ten minutes of injury time are nowhere near the record most sources cite, which is held by Paul Alcock, who added almost 23 minutes to the first half of a game between Bristol City and Brentford in August 2000.

You begin to understand why he did so when you read the the BBC's match report: 'Brentford's Lloyd Owusu suffered a neck injury as three players were stretchered off in the 2-2 draw between Bristol City and Brentford at Ashton Gate.'

Yet it's quite possible that the real record holder is Welshman Clive Thomas. According to Jack Rollin's book *More Soccer Shorts*, he 'once added three quarters of an hour to normal playing time'. The explanation was Thomas's legendary penchant for accuracy. 'It was a Boys Club match on the top of a mountain at Blaengwynfi,' explains Rollin, 'and every time the ball went out of play it rolled down the mountainside.'

Thomas must have painstakingly timed every single break in play, displaying the same meticulousness with which he once disallowed Zico's headed winner from a corner against Sweden in the 1978 World Cup. There was, Thomas decided,

The punctilious Welshman Clive Thomas blows for full time a split second before Zico's phantom winner for Brazil against Sweden.

enough time on the clock for Nelinho to take the corner but in the two seconds that elapsed between the kick and Zico heading home, Thomas blew for full time. (An often-overlooked footnote to this infamous story is that Thomas had added considerable stoppage time to the first 45 minutes during which – to Sweden's chagrin – Reinaldo scored Brazil's equaliser. And it all turned out alright for Brazil, who went on to win the World Cup, in its first ever penalty shoot-out.)

Still, many supporters might prefer such punctiliousness to the more laissez-faire brand of timekeeping which has led to the phenomenon known as Fergie Time: the time referees were popularly believed to add on at Old Trafford if Manchester United were behind because they were terrified of Sir Alex Ferguson. Depending which data you read, Fergie Time is either scientifically proven – one study quoted by *The Guardian* found that injury time at United's home games from 2006–07 to September 2009 was, on average, 65.8 seconds longer if they did not have the lead than when they did – or a media myth fuelled by the paranoia of losing teams. An Opta comparison of injury times in the 2011–12 Premier League revealed that the team that benefitted from the most added time was ... Wigan Athletic, with an average playing time at home of 96 minutes 12 seconds.

Research on 750 matches in Spain's la Liga by Natxo Palacious-Huerta, a professor at the London School of Economics, and Luis Garicano and Canice Prendergast, suggests this phenomenon was not limited to northwest England. They found that if a home team was ahead in a close match in la Liga, referees added an average of two minutes. But if a home team was behind in a close match, the average added time stretched to four minutes. So Fergie Time is probably a benefit enjoyed by most managers on their own turf. Indeed, Manchester City's Sergio Agüero scored the goal that snatched the 2011–12 title from United in the 94th minute, prompting the overjoyed home fans to sing 'We won it in Fergie Time!'

⚽ What is the furthest a team has travelled for a domestic cup tie?

The reason this is hard to answer is that you can't take the easy route. You cannot pick a really big country like Australia and simply check if Perth Glory, on the west coast, have ever travelled to Brisbane Roar, on the east coast – 2,240 miles as the crow flies. Because what counts here is not just who played whom but where. The Supercoppa Italiana, for instance, the Italian version of the Charity Shield, has been staged in places as far away from Italy as Washington DC, Tripoli and Beijing.

Then there is one very special case – France. What makes this country's domestic competitions so unusual is that the clubs from the French overseas territories – from such far-flung places as Tahiti, New Caledonia, French Guyana, Guadeloupe, Martinique, Mayotte, Tahiti and Réunion – are considered French teams. Naturally, their clubs cannot compete in the French league, but there are regional championships and the respective winners used to play for a trophy known as the Outremer Champions Cup. It was always staged in France, so that it wasn't unusual for clubs from Réunion or Martinique to fly to Paris to play each other. (This competition was replaced in 2008, by one involving national teams.)

Clubs from the territories still compete in the Coupe de France. This competition is notoriously drawn-out – there are eight rounds before the clubs from the French First Division even enter – precisely because so many teams take part. The winners of the regional cups of the overseas departments and territories join the regular Coupe de France in the seventh round and can be drawn against any club from France.

Over the years, some of the journeys have been so long the footballers must have felt like explorers. The longest one we have found took place in 1976, when Nickel Nouméa from New Caledonia were drawn against third-division club AS Corbeil. Since the match was played in Saint-Ouen, in the suburbs of Paris, the visitors had to cover 10,412 miles. One way, of course. (They lost 3-0.)

The farthest a team from an overseas territory has progressed in this competition is the round of 32, or the ninth round, back in 1994–95. The club in question was La Saint-Louisienne from the Réunion island in the Indian Ocean. In the seventh round, La Saint-Louisienne covered 5,817 miles to reach Melun in France, where they beat Third Division side SA Epinal 3-1. One round later, Ligue 2 club Chamois Niortais travelled 5,829 miles to Saint-Louis to be defeated on penalties by La Saint-Louisienne. It took a Ligue 1 side to stop the minnows' heroic progress: AS Cannes (just 5,428 miles from Réunion) won 2-0 on this island in the Indian Ocean.

Culture

⚽ **Can footballers act and can actors play football?**

In 1920, British director George Berthold Samuelson directed a movie called *The Winning Goal*. No copy has survived and the British Film Institute doesn't even have a proper synopsis. Yet several footballers featured in this movie, the most famous being Jack Cock. The first Cornishman to play for England, Cock was a flamboyant character with a fine tenor voice and the looks of a natural celluloid hero. But he didn't really get to flex his acting muscles as the film was based around the fictional team Blackton Rovers – and Cock appeared as himself.

Then again, maybe players should have followed the example of Cock and Meredith. Because with a very few exceptions – notably Eric Cantona and Vinnie Jones – footballers tend to make fools of themselves when they try to act.

Mind you, footballers trying to act are no worse than, to pluck a name at random out of the air, Sylvester Stallone trying to convince as a footballer. In John Huston's *Escape To Victory* Stallone plays a goalkeeper in the POW team intent on both defeating the Germans (at football) and escaping. An early script had Stallone scoring the winning goal in the match but that scenario was rejected by the footballers involved (Pelé, Bobby Moore, Ossie Ardiles) and thereafter the once and future Rocky Balboa seemed to lose interest in his role.

As perfunctory as Sly's performance may have been, he was a cut above Will Ferrell's caffeine-addicted, hypercom-

Thursday 6 August at 8.00p.m.
EMBASSY CINEMA, VALLETTA

LORIMAR PRESENTS A FREDDIE FIELDS PRODUCTION A JOHN HUSTON FILM
SYLVESTER STALLONE
MICHAEL CAINE MAX VON SYDOW PELÉ
"ESCAPE TO VICTORY"

All proceeds in aid of
INSPIRE (The Eden and Razzett Foundation)
helping over 1000 children and adults
with disabilities & their families.
Price of Admission: €10 (including Reception)
Tickets available from Embassy Cinema, Inspire Premises

petitive youth team coach in *Kicking And Screaming* (2005); while Ferrell, in turn, out-acted John Lynch, who was dismally dull as George Best in the prosaically-titled *Best* (2000). El Beatle is far more interesting as the inspiration for Hellmuth Costard's *Football Like Never Before*, which, through the alchemy of Costard's off-the-wall sensibility, spins a routine fixture between Manchester United and Coventry City into a compellingly odd documentary, setting a precedent for the intriguing but more conventional portrait of Zizou in *Zidane* by Douglas Gordon and Philippe Parreno.

The perils of footballers stepping too far out of their comfort zone are illustrated by *Montana Tap* (originally entitled *Potato Fritz*), described by the critic Joe Hembus as a 'mystery cum comedy cum western'. Released in 1975, Peter Schamoni's film is not very good, but not trashy either, which is why it's not even regarded as a cult classic. Starring Hardy Krüger and Stephen Boyd, the film is chiefly remembered because 1974 World Cup winner Paul Breitner has a supporting role as the US Cavalry's Sergeant Stark. His dialogue had to be rerecorded and even though he's supposed to be a soldier, Breitner sports his trademark afro and beard. At least he didn't fall off the horse.

Seeing Breitner on horseback was nothing compared to the shock that awaited Germans on 9 January 1999. On that Sunday evening, the 403rd episode of the hugely popular crime series *Tatort* was televised. It opens with a scene, set at night, in which a small boy releases his pet rabbit into the garden, then closes the French window and walks into the kitchen. He turns on the gas stove, blocks the knobs so that gas keeps emitting, lights a candle, then walks back into his room and climbs into bed. A few moments later, a neighbour knocks on the French door. The boy's father pulls on a bathrobe and opens the French window. The neighbour steps into the living room. He is cradling the rabbit in his arms. 'I found your rabbit near my front door,' he says. Then he sniffs. 'It smells of gas,' he says. The man in the bathrobe runs into the kitchen, realises what is happening and hastily blows out the candle before turning off the stove.

The neighbour strolls into the kitchen, still holding the rabbit. 'What is going on here? Are you trying to kill us all?' he says in the monotonous tone of someone who knows they can't act and approaches each line as a damage limitation exercise. The father blames incompetent heating engineers. The neighbour shakes his head in a robotic, unnatural manner. 'Sue them,' he says. 'Such people have taken up the wrong profession.' Then he hands over the rabbit. 'Give him an extra carrot,' he says. 'He's saved all our lives.'

The neighbour is none other than Berti Vogts, another 1974 World Cup winner. At that time, he was between jobs. Three years later, he became Scotland manager, a role in which, according to the Tartan Army, he was only slightly more convincing.

And so to the stars. Before Cantona and Jones, the one footballer who could be said to have enjoyed a real movie career was Dundee United inside-left Neil Paterson – a man who was the first amateur to captain a professional side in Britain but never wanted to earn a living from the game. This was a smart call, financially, because he was hired by DC Thomson as a sports journalist, wrote several novels and stories and, in 1953, adapted his own tale *The Kidnappers* for the cinema. Five years later he won an Oscar for his screenplay of John Braine's novel *Room At The Top*. He couldn't make it to the ceremony so he stayed up, at home with his family in Crieff, Perthshire, waiting for a call to tell him whether he'd won.

Eric Cantona's movie career has now lasted longer than his time in football. He made his first appearance in a French comedy in 1995 and has surfaced in more than a dozen films since then, including a fine cameo as the French ambassador at the court of Cate Blanchett in *Elizabeth*, and a starring role as Monsieur Cantona in Ken Loach's *Looking for Eric*.

Vinnie Jones was one of the leading lights in Wimbledon's Crazy Gang (a group of maverick footballers who were, to adapt one of Tommy Docherty's famous remarks, legends in their own minds), and his movie career has built on his hardman image. He played the enforcer Big Chris in *Lock, Stock and Two Smoking Barrels*, and was cast in Guy Ritchie's follow-up *Snatch*. In 2000, he had a lot of screen time as the villainous The Sphinx in *Gone In 60 Seconds*. Although Jones insisted he was inspired by Anthony Hopkins' Hannibal Lecter, the *Daily Mail* said that he recited his one line of dialogue with the 'ease and spontaneity of Sylvester Stallone reciting Book Six of *Paradise Lost*.' A limited repertoire of expressions hasn't stopped Jones appearing in more than fifty movies.

⚽ Who was the first team to wear advertising on their shirts?

Kettering Town is the usual answer. The non-league side turned out against Bath City on 24 January 1976 with the words 'Kettering Tyres' emblazoned in white lettering on their shirts. The four-figure sponsorship deal had been masterminded by club chief executive and manager Derek Dougan, the Wolves icon, but he soon began to reconsider when the FA threatened the club with a four-figure fine, saying it had banned the idea in 1972. After complaining that the 'petty-minded bureaucrats' hadn't put their ban in writing, the Doog gave in – after his idea about changing the lettering to 'Kettering T' had been nixed. He must have wondered what all the fuss was about when the ban was lifted five years later and Liverpool broke new ground by wearing Hitachi-sponsored shirts in 1978.

The Reds were the first to pioneer this commercialisation in England but such deals had been allowed in the Bundesliga since 1974–75. That was a response to the rescue of Eintracht Braunschweig by Günter Mast, the owner of Jägermeister liqueur. The club logo was a lion but after a DM 100,000 payment, the lion was ousted by the Jägermeister deer in time for the side's Bundesliga match against Schalke on 24 March 1973.

Mast may have been inspired by the initiative of Austrian brewer Manfred Mautner Markhof who, just before the start of the 1966–67 season, decided to sponsor Austria Wien. The beer glass trademark of Markhof's Schwechater beer was at the centre of their purple shirts. They were even more surprised to be handed new regulations which stipulated, at the sponsor's insistence, that 'long hair will not be permitted on the field of play. A decent haircut is mandatory for all players.'

In the European game, Austria Wien pioneered what some see as a sacrilegious act and others defend as a necessary commercialisation. But there is a possibility that the Uruguayan giants Peñarol experimented with shirt sponsorship in the mid-1950s. The club cite ANDA in 1984 as their first official sponsor but there is a story that, back in the mid-1950s, their

World Cup-winning hero Obdulio Varela refused to wear a sponsored shirt explaining (according to Galeano's *Football In Sunshine And Shadow*): 'They used to drag us blacks around by rings in our noses. Those days are gone.' According to this story, ten Peñarol players took to the field wearing the new shirt, with advertising, while club legend Varela, in his last season, wore the old, unsullied one.

⚽ Who was the only footballer to sing on the same bill as The Beatles?

Colin Grainger, aka The Singing Winger, shared a stage with the Fab Four on 13 June 1963 at Manchester's Southern Sporting Club. Grainger recalled: 'The Beatles were on the verge of becoming superstars but they had to take the booking because they had signed the contract a year before. I remember John Lennon, Paul McCartney and George Harrison as serious young men and professional, but Ringo Starr messed about, playing with Dinky cars on the floor. You knew then they were special, so it was a privilege to be on the same bill.'

Once hailed as one of the fastest men in football, Grainger grew up idolising Al Jolson and Mario Lanza. As he rose through the ranks in the 1950s, he admitted: 'Some of the biggest names in football say I'm a fool for not giving up soccer and concentrating on singing. They know that I can earn £100 for singing a few songs in variety theatres.' (Bear in mind that, by the end of the 1950s, the maximum wage for footballers was just £20 a week.)

Yet Grainger stuck at it, playing for seven clubs – notably Sheffield United and Sunderland – in a 16-year career and winning seven caps. His potted biography in the matchday programme for his last international, against Scotland in

Albert Stubbins of Sgt. Pepper fame cleaning his boots. 'It was such a John name,' Paul McCartney recalled, 'Al-bert Stub-bins. It just sounded right.'

April 1957, noted that he 'has great potentialities as a modern popular singer and has made a record'. When he hung up his boots, he turned to 'crooning' full-time, doing reasonably entertaining impersonations of the likes of Jolson, Engelbert Humperdinck and Elvis Presley.

Grainger may have shared the bill with the Beatles but he didn't make the cover of Sgt. Pepper. That honour was reserved for Albert Stubbins, who appears just behind

Marlene Dietrich, to the right of George Harrison. In his biography of the group, Hunter Davies wrote: 'I had always been slightly disappointed that none of the Beatles were interested in sport at all, least of all football. In the end, John stuck in Albert Stubbins, a folk name from his childhood.' Stubbins, who had scored 83 goals in 146 games for Liverpool, didn't realise he had been honoured until he received a copy of the album with a note: 'Well done Albert, for all those glorious years in football. Long may you bob and weave.' This shouldn't be taken as an informed analysis of Stubbins' playing style.

The other Beatles-related football mystery that will probably never be solved is why, given the apathy described above, Matt Busby is namechecked in a Beatles lyric. The song 'Dig It', on the *Let It Be* album, includes the lines, 'Like the FBI and the CIA/And the BBC/B.B. King/And Doris Day/Matt Busby/Dig it dig it'. The legendary Scot had played for Liverpool before any of the Beatles were born but, as Barney Ronay suggests in his book on managers, he may just be mentioned because by 1970, when the song was written, 'Busby already had the air of an ancient, much valued institution, something stoical and comforting, like the World Service'.

⚽ Do bogey teams really exist?

David Runciman, who occasionally writes about football matters in the *London Review of Books*, would probably suggest that the idea of a bogey team – along with the popular myth that the Manager of the Month award is a curse – merely reflect our inability 'to distinguish between statistically meaningless sequences and the march of destiny'. Over time, whatever fans might like to think, results tend to revert to an average.

And yet there are some strange sequences of results that suggest something irrational is going on. Between early 1990 and late 2006, Spurs played Chelsea no less than 37 times in all competitions, both home and away, but could win only one of these games – and that was a League Cup match. This kind of run can become self-perpetuating with the pre-match build-up in the media planting the thought in Spurs players' minds that they are unlikely to beat Chelsea. Once this idea takes hold, it may be more likely to come true.

Given the clubs' respective fortunes over that period, Spurs' barren streak might not seem that surprising. Spurs won just two trophies in that time (the FA Cup in 1991 and the League Cup in 1999), while Chelsea won seven (two Premier League titles, two FA Cups, two League Cups and the Cup Winners Cup). The Blues also finished above their London rivals in the league 13 times in the 18 seasons affected by this run. What was so intriguing about Spurs' run is that they couldn't win home or away. It is far more common for teams to suffer some kind of block when they return to a particular ground.

Spurs themselves also failed to win in 40 attempts at Anfield between 1912 and 1985. And for thirty years, Borussia Mönchengladbach just couldn't scrape a win away to Bayern Munich. Now, you could say it's hard for anyone to win at Bayern, but Gladbach's winless streak lasted from 1965, the year both teams were promoted to the Bundesliga, until 1995. In many of those 30 years, Borussia had a great team, winning the title five times and reaching five European finals (winning the UEFA Cup in 1975 and 1979). Ironically, when they finally broke their duck they did so with one future Bayern star in the side (Patrik Andersson), one former (Michael Sternkopf) and one future and former (Stefan Effenberg).

These curses may have been lifted, but another jinx is still alive and well. In Mexico, Club Deportivo Guadalajara

(Chivas) and Club Universidad Nacional (Pumas) are two of the best teams, having won 18 league titles between them. On 7 February 1982, a Manuel Negrete goal in the 89th minute secured a win for Pumas away at Chivas's Jalisco ground. They haven't won there since. The streak, which now enters its fourth decade, is even odder since Mexico introduced the Apertura/Clausura system in the mid-1990s, which means the league crowns a winter and a summer champion and teams play each other four times instead of just twice. At the time of writing, Pumas have gone 34 matches away at Chivas without a win.

The strange thing is that the Estadio Jalisco is home to three other Mexican teams, namely Atlas, Oro and Universidad de Guadalajara. The Pumas can defeat any of these sides at the Jalisco – and they can beat Chivas at home. It's just the combination of playing Chivas at the Jalisco that undoes them.

⚽ Why do Brazil wear yellow shirts with green trim and blue shorts?

The question sounds absurd. Yellow, green and blue are the colours of the Brazilian national flag, so the choice seems perfectly natural – as indeed it is, but strip and flag were not always in glorious unison.

In 1950, Brazil hosted – and expected to win – the World Cup. For the one and only time, the tournament was played in two group stages so there was no official final as such, but Brazil's clash with Uruguay on 16 July 1950 would decide who won the Jules Rimet trophy. Rimet himself, the French inventor of this tournament, had already written a speech congratulating Brazil on winning. The Brazilian FA had commissioned 22 gold medals with the players' names imprinted on them. Brazilian coach Flávio Costa tried to fight such over-confidence, warning: 'The Uruguayan team has always disturbed the slumbers of Brazilian footballers. I'm afraid that my players will take the field on Sunday as though they already had the championship shield sewn on their jerseys. It isn't an exhibition game. It is a match like any other, only harder.'

Such cautionary words went largely unheeded and, as the players lined up in the Maracanã, in front of a crowd of 200,000 (280 of whom came from Uruguay), the governor of the state of Rio addressed the players with a speech that began: 'You Brazilians, whom I consider victors of the tournament … you players who in less than a few hours will be acclaimed by millions of your compatriots'.

Such hubris had its just reward. The shock, when Brazil lost 2-1 to Uruguay, was so profound, so seismic, that, as Brazilian novelist Carlos Heitor Cony put it, 'Survivors of that cruel afternoon believed they would never again be happy.' As the sadness turned to anger, a national search for scapegoats began. Goalkeeper Moacyr Barbosa would never be forgiven for conceding Uruguay's winner. Twenty years later, he was spotted out shopping and a woman turned to her son and said: 'Look at him, he's the man who made Brazil cry.' Brazilian journalist Roberto Muylaert revealed in his book on the keeper that, in 1963, Barbosa invited friends to a barbecue where the wood he was burning turned out to be the very goalposts he had stood between in 1950, which had just been rendered obsolete by FIFA regulations.

For a nation that was, in Cony's words, 'drenched with pain', persecuting the keeper could never salve the wound. So Brazilians did what many coaches, players and supporters have done: they blamed the kit. At that time, Brazil wore white shirts with a blue collar. After the defeat, as Alex Bellos

The wrong shirts. Barbosa concedes the fateful goal, scored by Ghiggia.

says in his book *Futebol*, 'they were deemed not sufficiently nationalistic'. For Rio paper *Correio da Manhã,* the white strip suffered from a "psychological and moral lack of symbolism".'

So a competition was launched to create a kit, drawing on the colours of the national flag, that Brazil could wear in the 1954 World Cup. Ironically, given the media's talk of nationalism and symbolism, the competition was won by Uruguayan illustrator Aldyr Garcia Schlee, who entered for a laugh but ending up defining one of the most famous, romantic strips football has ever known. So you could say that Brazil wear yellow, green and blue because they lost to Uruguay.

This reaction is extreme – but not unusual. Bayern once invented a kit to secure a long-awaited win over Kaiserslautern. In the 1970s and early 1980s, the Roten went ten games without a win there, prompting Breitner to remark that Bayern should spare themselves the journey 'and just send them the points by mail'. In November 1983, business manager Uli Hoeness took drastic action, commissioning a custom-made kit Bayern had never worn before and would never wear again. In these unusual colours, Bayern finally enjoyed some luck at Kaiserslautern's Betzenberg ground, with their keeper Jean-Marie Pfaff saving a penalty and Klaus Augenthaler scoring the only goal for the visitors. Bayern usually played in red or white, but for this match, they wore yellow shirts, blue shorts and white socks. Hoeness believed that Brazil's kit would guarantee success.

Sir Alex Ferguson would have understood. He ditched Manchester United's grey away shirts at half-time, when his team went 3-0 down against Southampton. 'The players couldn't pick each other out,' he explained. 'They said it was difficult to see their team-mates at distance when they lifted their heads. It was nothing to do with superstition.' It didn't make much difference on the day as Southampton won 6-3, but the shirts were never used again.

Don Revie would have understood, too. Watching Real Madrid win the 1960 European Cup final 7-3, he decided, when he became Leeds United manager in 1961, that he wanted his new team to play in the same all-white strip. Such a superstitious soul that he nursed a mysterious fear of ornamental elephants, Revie believed in his vision so much that he wanted the fans to share in it and insisted that Admiral make replica kits, the first such deal in British football.

Real Madrid are so synonymous with the all-white kit that it is often forgotten that they once dared to change their colours. In the 1920s, Real stars Perico Escobal and Félix Quesada watched London's Corinthians while travelling in England. The players were so impressed by the Corinthians' fair play and elegance that, when they returned to Madrid, they persuaded club president Pedro Parages that Real should wear black shorts, just like the Londoners, for the 1925–26 season. Parages was willing to give it a go but after two bad defeats in the semi-finals of the Spanish Cup to Barcelona – including a 5-1 thrashing in Madrid that must have hurt deeply – he decided that the black shorts were bad luck. The team reverted to playing in white and have been, if you consider only their home kit, *los blancos* ever since.

⚽ What is the world's longest-running football comic?

Let's clarify our terms. Roy Race, the hero of Melchester Rovers, had his own strip in *Tiger* in 1954 but only starred in his own all-football comic between 1976 and 1995. In other words, for 19 years. That is some feat but Race's organ looks like a one-season wonder when compared to *Los Barrabases*, the Chilean football comic which, in four interrupted incarnations, lasted for 32 years and is still published to mark the really big tournaments.

Created by estate agent Guido Vallejos ('I was hopeless at football so I found it easier to draw it'), *Barrabases* first appeared in August 1954 when Vallejos invested a big commission and some money borrowed from his wife in a printing press. The title, which could roughly be translated as rascals or pranksters, refers to a mischief-making youth team coached by a Mr Pipa. The first run of 10,000 copies, distributed only in Santiago and Valparaiso, sold out and the circulation grew to 100,000 as the

comic went from fortnightly to weekly. The Barrabases even got their radio show in which football presenter Máximo Claveriá commentated on the team's fictitious games.

Like Ajax, the Barrabases traditionally favoured 4-3-3. Unlike Ajax, they relied on a loveable Chilean mongrel, team mascot Rasca, to get them out of many nasty scrapes. In one instalment, Mr Pipa's boys took on Colo-Colo, Chile's most successful and popular team. For this prestige fixture, Pipa sent for reinforcements, drafting in a legendary, super-jumping Scottish-Chilean goalkeeper called Sapo Livington (*sapo* means toad).

The early issues featured, in a rather post-modern conceit, *El Camote* (The Muddle), a sports newspaper for kids, which reported on Barrabases' performance in the local championship. After a tournament in 1960, the paper wrote of 'great discontent among the fans. After sensational victories over Boca Juniors and the Spanish children's national side, Los Barrabases have failed. The president Rucedino Tapilla is saying nothing … Mr Pipa under a cloud.'

The team was the centrepiece of the comic, in their heyday filling at least half the issue. The other pages were filled with short stories about various characters from different sports. The comic's publishing history is a bit hazy but the first incarnation lasted until 1961. Relaunched in 1968, revamped in 1970, the title closed again in 1973 (though not before Chilean footballer Carlos Reinoso bought the licence to launch it in Mexico where he was playing for Club America). After another failed comeback, *Los Barrabases* was back in 1989. The team now had the whole comic to themselves and, though the drawings weren't as good, the new formula worked. Mr Pipa's team celebrated their fiftieth anniversary with a match against Real Madrid's galacticos in 2004 and, even though the title closed in 2006, special editions have since been published to mark the 2010 World Cup and the 2011 Copa America.

Los Barrabases may have shown the most stamina but they were not the first. From 1922 until the outbreak of the Spanish Civil War in 1936, young Catalan football fans thrilled to the humour and drawings in *Xut!* ('Shoot!'), a comic created by artist Valentí Castanya in which the spritely, grandfatherly hero Avi became a symbol of Barcelona football club. Now regarded as a crucial cultural record of Catalona in the 1920s and 1930s, *Xut!* struck such a chord that decades later one *Blaugrana*, Joan Casals, started going to games dressed as Avi. In 1992, after Barcelona had won the European Cup, he famously proclaimed that he would shave his beard off if the club won the competition again. He kept his promise in 2006. His devotion to Castanya's comic is one reason why Barcelona is one of the few clubs not to have a man in a fake animal suit as a mascot.

Avi depicted as a *caganero*, or shitting man. Catalans have a tradition of placing these earthy statuettes amid their nativity cribs.

⚽ Who was the greatest ever comic strip football hero?

A supremely gifted right-winger called Eric Castel. At least that was how he was known in Spain, France and Belgium. In the Netherlands they knew him as Ronnie Hansen, in Germany he was Kai Falke. For simplicity, we'll call him Castel.

Inspired by the imminent opportunity provided by the 1974 World Cup, Franco-Belgian illustrator Raymond Reding created a supposedly one-off football comic strip for the German magazine *Zack*. It centred on Falke, the player-manager of a company team, who was signed by Barcelona. That hugely implausible event aside, the strip had little in common with the most famous English football comic, the usually improbable adventures of Roy of the Rovers.

Reding was an artist whose precise, realistic drawings were rich in detail. His stories were as famed for their impressive renderings of buildings and stadiums as for their football action. Reding was anxious to avoid the kind of over-the-top storylines so popular in other football strips. Castel was outstanding but unlike Melchester Rovers hero Roy Race, he was no superman, did not get shot by a lone gunman and never strengthened his squad by signing two members of Spandau Ballet. Castel's Barcelona played realistic games against real-life clubs. It meant that Castel appealed to adults as much as to kids.

Reding resurrected his hero in 1979 for a full-length album, the first of 15 over the next 13 years. Gradually, Castel's story came to be regarded as the best football strip in the world. In 2004, five years after Reding's death, the Catalan company Ramon Usall published a book on the strip that declared that Castel embodied Catalan values. In his foreword, Joan Laporta, then Barcelona's club president, said: 'Eric Castel was one of the best signings in Barça's history.'

Move over, Messi. Barça's all-time top signing was Eric Castel.

Apart from the Rovers' Roy Race, Castel's rivals in Britain would include Billy Dane, the boy who became a brilliant footballer when he put on a pair of magic boots, found in his gran's attic, worn decades before by legendary striker Charles 'Dead Shot' Keen. This simple premise proved so enduring that *Billy's Boots* were featured in *Tiger, Scorcher, Eagle, Roy of the Rovers, Total Football,* in the German comic Kobra and (as Billi Boot) in Bengali magazine *Shuktaara*.

Billy Dane was also an inspirations for *Viz* magazine's Billy The Fish, which for many Brits of a certain age was the most iconic comic strip football hero of all. Fulchester United goalkeeper Billy Thomson found it easier to leap like a salmon because he was half-man, half-fish and *Viz*'s skewering of Roy of the Rovers led to such storylines as Shakin' Stevens join-ing United. Yet the strip developed a surreal identity of its own, with an invisible striker (Johnny X, who had vanished after his father died) and a Professor Wolfgang Schnell B.Sc., Ph.D. whose use of a calculator, charts and a geometry set to calculate the best trajectory for a shot eerily prefigures today's number-crunching, stat-driven, Optastic punditry.

⚽ Why are corner flags so important?

When Cameroon's Roger Milla ran over to the corner flag to celebrate his opening goal against Romania at the 1990 World Cup, the world watched in delight – and a trend was born. That was the moment football players discovered the manifold possibilities of using a corner flag as a prop. Many of them no longer treat it as respectfully as Milla. Some goalscorers have taken to ripping the flag out of its socket, others give it a flying kick. A nadir was possibly reached when Finidi George unleashed a bizarre urinating-dog celebration after he had scored against Greece at USA 94.

But you wonder if any of these celebrants are aware of the risk involved, because if a corner flag is broken and cannot be repaired or replaced the referee has to abandon the game. Yes, that's how important the corner flags are. If they happen to be missing, the beginning of a game will have to be delayed until they arrive (as happened most famously in the 1974 World Cup final, which referee Jack Taylor couldn't start at the appointed time because the corners were empty). And if anything happens to one of the four flagposts during a game, play has to be stopped. As referee Dennis Wickham explains: 'In a professional match, another flag would likely be found. But corner flags are mandatory under the laws of the game. If a flag cannot be found (or safely assembled) the letter of the law would prevail, and the match would be abandoned.'

The question is: why? Why are the flags deemed so important that you cannot play football without them? After all, they don't do much. They mark the corners of the field of play – but so do the line markings. They are supposed to help the linesman decide whether a ball that goes out of play near the corner has crossed the touchline or the goal line but this isn't a common dilemma for officials and only helps them distinguish a corner or a goal kick from a throw-in. In comparison, the flags that used to mark the halfway line at many grounds have virtually disappeared, making way for fourth officials (who first appeared at a major tournament at the 1998 World Cup), TV cameras and technical areas (introduced into the laws of the game in 1994). These flags were only ever optional in the rules ('Flagposts may also be placed at each end of the halfway line'), even though they help the referee decide whether a player is offside or not. (You're never offside in your own half.)

In a game like field hockey – played on a similar pitch with the same kind of corner rules – the corner flags are nowhere near as sacred (if both teams are happy with this, the referee can start a game without them), even though the ball is a lot smaller and harder to follow. Since there is no immediately obvious, plausible explanation for the disproportionate importance of a corner flag in football, it seems likely we're dealing with a remnant of the game's past.

The answer may be found in the original rules of the Football Association as drawn up in 1863. The very first one said: 'The maximum length of the ground shall be 200 yards, the maximum breadth shall be 100 yards, the length and breadth shall be marked off with flags; and the goal shall be defined by two upright posts, eight yards apart, without any tape or bar across them.' Notice the rule doesn't mention the need for a crossbar or any line markings. That's because there were none for many decades. Only in 1891 did the rules require goal lines and touchlines to be marked. So, for almost three decades, the corner flags were the only marks that told you where the pitch began or ended. Actually, together with the four goalposts they were the only objects that defined the field of play. They may be superfluous today but it's hard to imagine the game without them.

⚽ What exactly is a derby?

Fans across the world use the English term *derby* (generally pronounced *der*-by rather than *dar*-by) for a local rivalry. The oddest, geographically, has to be the inter-continental clash between Galatasaray and Fenerbahçe, as the former are based in the European part of Istanbul, the latter on the Asian side of the Bosphorus strait. The oldest is usually said to be the Trentside one, first played on 23 March 1866, between Nottingham Forest (who had only switched to football from the Gaelic sport of shinty the year before) and Notts County. The match is usually said to have ended 0-0.

Just 300 yards (and the river Trent) separate Forest's City Ground from Notts County's Meadow Lane, while

Galatasaray and Fenerbahçe's stadiums are only nine miles apart. But not every club competing a derby is quite so lucky. Whenever Kaliningrad's Baltika on the Russian coast are promoted to the country's top flight – it last happened in 1995 – the players are probably ambivalent about such success. In the Russian top flight, the club closest to Baltika is Zenit St Petersburg, some 620 miles to the north.

Even that would seem a jaunt to footballers in Perth, on the west coast of Australia. When the optimistically monikered Perth Glory steel themselves for a match with their nearest rivals, they have a 1,322 mile schlep to Adelaide United. However, both Australian clubs prefer to acknowledge other derbies. Perth's players, officials and fans focus on the so-called Distance Derby with Wellington Phoenix, 3,270 miles away in New Zealand.

This derby started as a joke but acquired juice when the clubs vied for third in the A League in 2011–12. Adelaide's fiercest rivalry is the Cross-Border Derby with Melbourne Victory. As the name suggests, this fixture's importance has been fuelled by the fierce, historic rivalry between South Australia (where United are based) and Victoria (home to Victory). The first Cross-Border Derby match was only played in 2005 but the rivalry intensified after an incident the following year when Adelaide's outspoken coach John Kosmina grabbed Melbourne skipper Kevin Muscat by the throat after the player had knocked Kosmina off his chair while trying to collect the ball. The incident inspired the Kosmina-Muscat Cup, awarded to the best team in their league encounters.

All of which might suggest that it doesn't really matter how old a derby is. Or how close the teams are. If fans pine for their own 'El Clasico', the Cross-Border Derby shows you just need to create one.

⚽ How effective is drinking as a motivational aid?

During the 1997–98 season, Barnsley's only Premier League campaign, the players went out for a night on the town. As German goalie Lars Leese recalls in his memoir *The Keeper Of Dreams*, he shocked midfielder Darren Sheridan by lighting up a Marlboro Light. Sheridan rebuked Leese, saying he shouldn't be smoking because he was a professional athlete. To which the keeper replied: 'Well, look at yourself.' Sheridan, who was about to down his sixth pint of the evening, had no idea what Leese was talking about.

Brian Clough would have been just as mystified. 'The key to preparation,' he said once, 'is relaxation.' So on the coach to Munich's Olympiastadion before the 1979 European Cup final, he urged the Nottingham Forest players to have a beer. He had tried the same tactic in March that year, the night before the League Cup final. 'We had everything we could possibly have wanted to drink. Bitter, lager, mild, champagne,' recalled striker Garry Birtles. 'There were people who could hardly stand by the time we went to bed.

Clough insisted on it. Archie Gemmill wanted to go to bed. He wouldn't let him.' The experiment succeeded – but only just. Forest were 1-0 down to Southampton at half-time but sobered up in time to win it 3-2. It turned out okay for the European Cup, too, with Forest beating Malmö 1-0.

Even in the 1970s, Clough's methods were unorthodox, but many managers turned a blind eye to players' drinking as long as they were sober on the training ground and on matchdays. Max Merkel, the great Austrian coach who won league titles in Austria, Germany and Spain, was once asked if his players were allowed a tipple. He replied: 'During training,

I once put all the drinkers into one team and the teetotallers into the other. The drinkers won the match at a canter. So I said, "Okay, keep on drinking".'

The first recorded evidence of concern that footballers were drinking too much is a ringing defence of the profession by Aston Villa forward Archie Hunter – in 1890. Challenging the 'impression abroad' that 'after every match the members [players] go to the nearest tavern and drink as hard as they can', he insisted they could drink only moderately because to do otherwise would be to damage their career. In the decades since, the careers of countless footballers – not just in Britain – have shown that wasn't quite the case. The roll call of only the most famous victims includes such names as Tony Adams, George Best, Hughie Gallacher, Garrincha, Jimmy Greaves, Ladislao Kubala, Diego Maradona (it wasn't just the cocaine, he was a bottle of whisky a night man), Socrates. And Paul Gascoigne.

Some old-school memoirs invest the players' hard drinking escapades with a tawdry glamour. The dismal reality is reflected more accurately in Ken Gallacher's biography of Jim Baxter. The gifted Scottish playmaker joined Sunderland in 1965 and when the move failed to revive his career, drank even more heavily than he had in Glasgow. As Gallacher notes, his Sunderland team-mates 'would gauge just how bad his night had been by how many times he threw up after his arrival.'

One of the most notorious alcohol-fuelled team bonding sessions took place at the China Jump Club in Hong Kong before England were due to host Euro 96. Although Paul Gascoigne pleaded in his autobiography, 'It was all a laugh, us letting our hair down before the Euro finals', the British tabloids profoundly disagreed, with the *Sun* calling Gascoigne a 'disgraced fool'. The England team had started out with Flaming Lamborghini cocktails and then noticed the 'dentist's chair'. If you sat in it, two barmen would come over and pour bottles of three different spirits down your neck. Teddy Sheringham was unlucky enough to be photographed getting the treatment and looked, as team-mate Stuart Pearce noted, more like Ollie Reed than a professional footballer.

The England players must have thought they had had the last laugh when they celebrated Gazza's sublime goal against Scotland. The England No. 8 passed the ball to himself over Colin Hendry's head and volleyed into the net. As Gazza lay prone on the pitch, his team-mates grabbed some bottles and squirted water into his open mouth, mimicking the dentist's chair incident and creating one of the most memorable goal celebrations in the history of the England team. The joy of that memory is tempered, now, by the knowledge of Gascoigne's terrible, subsequent struggles with alcohol.

It is rare for players to go as far as to have an inspirational tipple in the dressing room. Brazilian goal machine Arthur Friedenreich, whose goal won the Copa America in 1919, acquired a taste for beer and French brandy and liked a quick pick-me-up before he ran out on to the pitch. Hughie Gallacher, the outstanding Scottish forward of the 1920s and 1930s, once defended himself against accusations that he was drunk on the pitch by insisting he had used whisky as mouthwash.

Barcelona's Hungarian idol Ladislao Kubala, the club's all-time top scorer before Messi, once drank so much on a matchday that he could only play after being thrown into a shower and pumped with black coffee. That wasn't untypical: Kubala had been in an alcoholic haze when he arrived in Spain, too drunk to realise the train he thought was taking him to Madrid was heading to Barcelona. He scored 274 goals for the *Blaugranas* and was, according to Alfredo di Stéfano, the best ball juggler in the history of the game. Kubala remains a hero in Catalonia and Hungary even if, as time passes, his legend as a drinker is

The infamous dentist's chair celebration: Gazza gets the bottles from Steve McManaman, Alan Shearer and Jamie Redknapp.

in danger of overshadowing his fame as a footballer. Passing through customs once, he was asked to identify the two bottles of whisky he had declared on the form. The Hungarian star just pointed at his stomach.

This was the kind of lifestyle Sir Alex Ferguson fought against when he took over Manchester United in 1986, fuming that he had inherited a drinking club, not a football club. He soon purged the squad but didn't go quite as far as Arnold Hills, the Temperance Society member who changed the name of Thames Ironworks in 1900 to West Ham United. As a report in the *Morning Leader* noted: 'Mr A. F. Hills is very keen on playing a teetotal eleven next season.'

Hills never achieved his goal. Footballers still drink and defy medical science, coaches and the odds. Alcohol eventually did for Rudi Brunnenmeier, a fabulously gifted footballer who could, a trifle reductively, be known as the German George Best, but his career is as full of picaresque incidents as Kubala's. In the early hours of 1 September 1965, he was trying to weave his way home in Munich without hitting the concrete when he collided with a postman clutching a telegram. The German B team were due to face the Soviet Union later that day and he had been called up after a late injury. Still intoxicated, he made his way to the airport and flew to Cologne. He spent the afternoon in a hotel bed, trying to sleep off his hangover. Then he scored twice against the Soviet Union, hopped on a plane back to Munich and headed for the city's bars.

What is the point of dugouts?

Dugouts were originally dug into the ground so that the coaching staff (and, later, substitutes) sat below ground level. But that is an oddity in itself, for a dugout is perhaps the worst possible vantage point for football, given how often managers complain about their view even when they are sitting on a normal bench on the sidelines.

According to the book *Dugouts*, featuring photographs by David Bauckham of team shelters across Britain, the 'first dugout appeared at Aberdeen's ground, Pittodrie, in the early 1920s. Aberdeen's trainer at the time, Donald Colman, was a boxing and dancing enthusiast, obsessed with his players' footwork, who made meticulous notes during each game. Needing a dry notebook, he had Aberdeen build a sunken covered area at Pittodrie, thereafter known as the "dugout".'

This is a wonderful story, though it remains unclear why Colman's idiosyncratic, impractical and expensive invention should have become popular, especially since clubs didn't need a subs' bench at the time because there were no subs in football – and wouldn't be until the 1960s.

Baseball, on the other hand, has always had subs. Lots of them. And the word 'dugout' first appears in print in connection with baseball. *The Dickson Baseball Dictionary* gives the date as 17 October 1912 in the *New York Tribune*, but there seem to be earlier instances. The Library of Congress database reveals that, six days earlier, a piece in the *Washington Post* about pitcher Richard William 'Rube' Marquard began thus: 'Down in the dugout he sat, his lank legs crossed, his long arms dangling – a listless, indifferent man in whom no emotion was visible.'

When you look at the early baseball photographs in the Library of Congress, you discover a metamorphosis. In the latter years of the nineteenth century, the players not involved in the action sit on normal, spacious and sheltered benches, just like subs in football today. These benches are situated as near to home plate (where the batter stands to face the pitcher) as possible without interfering with play, as players coming from the bench usually do so to bat. Traditionally, the home team sits along the first base line, the visitors along the third base line. Gradually, these benches began to shrink. By 1902, some enclosures were so low players couldn't really sit upright. And by 1908, the first benches had been lowered into the ground so that the players' hips or knees were level with the field of play. In 1912, dugouts were so common that newspapers could use the term without having to explain it. It was also the year that an iconic image of New York Giants manager John McGraw was taken: he leans on the railing, observing the game, while his players sit behind and beneath him, in the dugout.

If even managers like McGraw couldn't see what they want from the dugout, why did clubs lower the benches in the first place? Some say it protected the players from foul balls routinely hit with considerable force down the first or third base line. It's more likely, though, that it was done because it helped club owners make money.

The most expensive seats in a baseball stadium are behind the home plate. If you have two sheds for players there, you are blocking the view for quite a few rows. Some clubs must have begun lowering the roof of the players' shelter to install more seats, until the players complained. That's when another solution was needed – and found. We don't know who first hit upon the idea of digging a hole for players, only that it wasn't Colman. Either he thought of it independently a few years later, or he was inspired by something he had heard or seen. Some Aberdeen legends, most notably Alex Jackson and Jock Hume, had spent some time in the American Soccer League in the early 1920s. Yet *Groundtastic* magazine, in a 2005 feature called 'Pyramid Passion', concluded 'it is more likely the idea came from one of Colman's coaching trips to Norway, where shelters were the norm due to the cold climate'.

⚽ When was the first fanzine?

The honour is often bestowed upon the venerable *When Saturday Comes*, concocted by Chelsea fan Mike Ticher while working in a London record shop in late 1985 and put into practice with the help of his work-mate, the Evertonian Andy Lyons, in March 1986. Yet the very first issue already mentioned 'another football magazine that refuses to sit back and watch while football dies', namely *Off The Ball*, published in Birmingham by a West Brom fan called Adrian

Goldberg. Many years later, Goldberg would be working for the BBC, which claimed he had 'founded Britain's first football fanzine'.

It's not true, though. Unbeknownst to them both at the time, Goldberg and Ticher had been beaten to the punch by Mike Harrison, who began putting out the Bradford City fanzine *The City Gent* in November 1984. In his Twitter profile, Harrison calls himself the 'editor of the oldest football fanzine in the UK', which is correct because *The City Gent* is still going strong.

But of course the oldest is not the first. That was a publication with a strong satirical bent called *FOUL*, started by a group of Cambridge University students and published between 1972 and 1976. One of the editors was Chris Lightbown. Many years later he said that *FOUL* came into being because 'football had simply not assimilated any of the social or cultural changes of the sixties. It was in a complete time warp'. In the same year in which Lightbown started *FOUL*, he also created a map for *Time Out* that illustrated football rivalries in London by allocating certain colours to certain clubs and showing in which boroughs these clubs' supporters were predominantly based. The map became somewhat famous nine years later when Desmond Morris published it in *The Soccer Tribe*.

Like all similar magazines that would follow, *FOUL* quickly built up a network of contributors, Eamon Dunphy among them. One reason the fanzine eventually folded was that Mike Langley, the then chief football writer for the *Sunday People*, threatened a lawsuit after a piece on soccer scribes. One of the original editors of the fanzine, Alan Stewart, became an investigative journalist and died when he was 35 after his car hit a landmine in southern Sudan. That was in late 1985, shortly before the fanzine boom kicked off.

● Who coined game of two halves, early doors and sick as a parrot?

In his book *Football Talk*, Peter Seddon says that, on 22 March 1978, after Liverpool had lost the League Cup final replay, defender Phil Thompson gave a post-match interview in which he admitted: 'I'm as sick as a parrot.'

This is, as Seddon carefully puts it, 'the first high-exposure usage of the phrase', though by the following year it was popular enough to appear in *Private Eye* – which is where the Oxford English Dictionary lists its first usage. Yet when John Bond died, at the age of 79, in December 2012, the *Daily Telegraph*, and several fan forums for Norwich City and Southampton, credited him with inventing the term. The *Telegraph* writer noted, 'Sick as a dog would have been the predictable cliché', before adding that they weren't sure if the substitution of the parrot was 'merely a blooper' or reflected 'the gift football has for reinvigorating the language'.

The association between gloom and parrots can be traced back to the Restoration dramatist Aphra Behn, in whose 1682 comedy *The False Count*, the maid tells her mistress, 'You are as melancholy as a sick parrot'. However, Bond or Thompson were more likely drawing, possibly sub-consciously, on Monty Python's iconic Dead Parrot sketch, which had been broadcast in 1969 and reappeared in their first movie *And Now For Something Completely Different*. Or was the Liverpool skipper, as Seddon also suggests, merely shortening the old Scouse saying 'sick as a parrot with a rubber beak'?

The first recorded use of the mysterious phrase 'early doors' in a footballing context is by that linguistic master, Brian Clough. In November 1979, the Nottingham Forest manager reflected in an interview on his relationship with some of his players: 'Early doors, it was vital that they liked me.' However, when popularised by champagne-swilling, jewellery-juggling manager and TV pundit 'Big' Ron Atkinson, it was taken to refer to the beginning of a game.

What exactly does early doors mean? Some say it refers to people who wait outside pub doors waiting for them to open (this may explain why Craig Cash called his cult sitcom *Early Doors*). Others claim that it refers to any situation where people are earlier than is customary – indeed, it is used by restaurant owners to promote 'early doors' pre-theatre menus. Seddon has a more cultured explanation: 'It originates from nineteenth-century theatrical jargon, theatre doors being opened early for patrons willing to pay a premium price to nab the best seats.' These were the so-called 'early doors' tickets.

Atkinson may not have coined 'early doors' but, with his eclectic mash-up of football jargon and the English language, he pioneered a new football language – 'Ronglish', if you will. Among his creations are 'lollipop' (when a player puts one foot over the ball and hits it with the outside of his other foot), 'Hollywood ball' (as in 'He could have played the easy pass but he had to try a Hollywood ball') and 'reducer' (using your most competitive defender to nullify a skilful opponent). After being caught on microphone racially abusing Marcel Desailly, Big Ron became Racist Ron. Yet in his heyday, Ronglish had a poetic resonance. His famous description of a penalty kick – 'Left peg. Back stick. Bish bosh.' – has the compressed eloquence of a Japanese haiku.

The origin of the phrase 'A game of two halves' is even more mysterious. In football parlance, it has become a clichéd way of observing that things can turn around. The ultimate example of a game of two halves is probably Liverpool's epic comeback in the 2005 UEFA Champions League final, having been 3-0 down at half-time. However, a recent discussion on the BBC World Service mooted that the original 'game of two halves' was the 1930 World Cup final in which a squabble over whose ball should be used – the point was not then covered in the tournament regulations – forced FIFA to decree that the Argentinian ball should be used in the first half and the Uruguayan in the second. For the record, Argentina won the half played with their ball 2-1, while the Uruguayan hosts edged the half in which their ball was used 3-1 to win the World Cup.

In Germany, they have their own variation on the game of two halves. Herberger, the most influential German coach of all time, used to remind players: 'A game lasts for 90 minutes'. The favoured German cliché, however, is 'In football, everything is possible'.

🌐 At which ground are visitors least likely to be insulted?

Germany's St. Pauli, based in the same part of Hamburg as the Reeperbahn, the famous red-light district, was a fairly normal football club until 1980. But then a street near the harbour gained national prominence, because the city wanted to knock down eight untenanted nineteenth-century houses. They attracted a colourful group of radical squatters – from punk rockers and students to political activists and eco-warriors. Many of them adopted St. Pauli as their team and they gradually transformed the club. This, in brief, is why the fans wave skull-and-crossbones flags, why you don't hear bland pop groups during half-time but street punks Cock Sparrer and why the team runs out to AC/DC's 'Hell's Bells'. And why they play the club anthem of the opposing team.

This is a sign of respect, fair play and signals that you are a guest, not an opponent. The same attitude informs a code of honour amongst the home support at St. Pauli's Millerntor

St. Pauli fans show their support for gay rights during their Bundesliga match with SC Paderborn 07 on 1 April 2013.

ground that blacklists songs and banners that put down the visiting team. Many away fans who visit St. Pauli don't feel bound by this rule and sing anti-St. Pauli songs. These are usually met from all stands with a round of pitiful applause that drips with sarcasm.

Asked what characterises the St. Pauli experience, the club's long-time director of football Helmut Schulte once said: 'Standing up to right-wing tendencies in a peaceful atmosphere, in which the opponent is our friend. Visiting teams and fans are not insulted. We don't take ourselves that seriously. Our fans support the team not when things are going well but when it needs support. These are just some of the special things that have become established here.'

It doesn't always work. On occasion you can hear fans sing songs about St. Pauli's local rivals, the much bigger Hamburg SV, that are not complimentary. But it works more often than not. When Hoffenheim travelled to St. Pauli in 2010, the home fans felt they should somehow make clear that they didn't approve of a club bankrolled by a billionaire. But their code of honour said they couldn't sing or do anything insulting. And so the St. Pauli fans silently unfolded a banner as the Hoffenheim team ran out. It read: 'We don't even ignore you'.

⚽ When was the first football magazine published?

On 22 November 1873, the first issue of a publication called *Goal: The Chronicle Of Football* appeared. For the first time, a British publisher had decided that the sport of association football was popular enough to warrant its own periodical. The publication barely lasted a season.

That hasn't stopped countless publishers betting on the same belief over the last 140 years. The first modern football magazine – containing the kinds of snippets, interviews and features we would recognise today – is generally said to be *Charles Buchan's Football Monthly* (1951–74). As a footballer with Sunderland and Arsenal, Buchan had lamented the lack of a 'weekly bible for the game' and, after hanging up his boots, decided to create one. In his first issue, he declared: 'Our object is to provide a publication that will be worthy of our national game and the grand sportsmen who play and watch it.' Stanley Matthews was the cover star of the first issue, in which the Marquess of Londonderry confessed he had become interested in football after hearing miners talk about it down the pits.

However, Buchan's tome was predated by *France Football* (launched in 1946) and *El Gráfico* (an Argentinian sports magazine with a strong focus on football, founded in 1919). Martin Westby, who runs the website Soccerbilia, suggests that the first modern football magazine was actually published in Germany. *Die Fussball-Woche* (The Football Week) was launched on 24 September 1923, though the title was published on newsprint and printed in black and white. The magazine was started in Berlin by a 30-year-old journalist called Kurt Stoof and ran until the end of the war, when the Allies shut down all publications. It took a while to get going again, because Stoof languished in a Soviet prison from 1945 to 1950 but on his release he revived his magazine in West Berlin and it's still going as a local football paper.

Yet *Kicker*, Germany's most famous football magazine, has been around even longer. Now idiosyncratically spelled with a lower-case 'k', *Kicker* is such an institution that calling it

the Bible of German football would be an understatement.
As with Stoof's *Die Fussball-Woche*, the history of *Kicker*
magazine is complicated because of the years after the war
when publications were closed and then relaunched. The
original *Kicker* was founded by the German football pioneer
Walther Bensemann in 1920 and the first issue was sold
on 14 July 1920, more than three years before *Die Fussball
Woche*. A magazine in a newspaper format, Bensemann's
Kicker started as a weekly (it now comes out every Monday
and Thursday) and covered every aspect of the game, even
history: the cover of the first issue depicted two Karlsruhe
teams from the 1890s.

Bensemann had discovered the joys of football while
attending a British private school in Switzerland in the 1880s.
The cosmopolitan son of a Jewish banker, he was instrumen-
tal in getting the game off the ground in Germany. Right from
the start, the idea behind *Kicker* was to take a broader view,

use foreign correspondents and carry smart, critical editorials. This was, Bensemann decided, the only way to distinguish his magazine from the competition.

Yes, *Kicker* had well-established competition in 1920 from *Fussball*, the official mouthpiece of the South German Football Association published by Eugen Seybold since 1911, and *Der Rasensport* (Field or Lawn Sport), launched in Berlin in 1902, whose subtitle was *Wochenschrift für die Interessen des Fussballsports* ('Weekly in the Interests of the Sport of Football'). Though the focus of *Der Rasensport* was on football, the editorial had a broad remit. In 1912, one issue featured detailed coverage of the season in England's Division Two. Five years later it bemoaned the fact that the 'blasé Berliners' didn't support their teams loudly enough. In 1929, the magazine became part of Stoof's *Fussball Woche*.

⚽ What is the lowest crowd for a top flight game?

Juventus have this pretty much sewn up. The *Bianconeri* have, according to polls, twelve million fans in Italy alone. Yet until they got their new stadium in 2011, their home games felt like some post-apocalyptic movie. The main reason for this was the Stadio delle Alpi, a cold (in every sense of the word) stadium with a running track and poor visibility, located on the outskirts of Turin. The club were saddled with this inhospitable home after the 1990 World Cup. For the 57 years before that they had been more happily ensconced downtown at the Stadio Comunale Vittorio Pozzo (formerly the Stadio Mussolini). The fans didn't appreciate the move.

On 27 October 1998, just 561 *tifosi* turned up for a Coppa Italia game between Juventus and Vicenza. With impressive understatement, Juve legend Alessio Tacchinardi, who was on the pitch that day, later said: 'We were tired, but maybe we would have found some energy if there had been more passion from the stands.' Then on 14 December 2001, another cup game, between Juve and Sampdoria, attracted (if that's the right word) 237 fans. The match kicked off at 6pm to suit television ('We won't give up a night match to play on a midweek afternoon again,' said the club's vice-president Roberto Bettega) and it was unusually cold that Wednesday. Still, as Amy Lawrence noted in the *Observer*: 'More than 237 would click through the turnstiles at Old Trafford even if there were an outbreak of bubonic plague – so the question must be asked: just what is Juventus's problem?' Well, as Tacchinardi put it: 'At the Stadio delle Alpi, the fans never really were the 12th man.'

The no-show by the *Bianconeri* unfaithful makes the Premier League's all-time low – 3,039 to watch an Everton side starring Peter Beardsley and Tony Cottee beat Wimbledon 3-1 on 26 January 1993 – look like a blockbuster crowd. However, the lowest-ever attendance for a Football League match is 13, the official tally for the crowd that watched Stockport County draw 0-0 with Leicester City at Old Trafford. There were extenuating circumstances – the game kicked off at 6.30pm and Stockport were forced to play at Old Trafford because their ground had been closed after irate fans had broken the window in the referee's dressing room after their team didn't get a stonewall penalty – and the real figure was probably higher. United had played earlier that day and it is estimated that 1,000 to 2,000 spectators from that match stayed behind to watch the second game for nothing.

Then again, it could have been worse for Juventus. If we ignore matches played behind closed doors (for example as a penalty for the home team), the lowest attendance for a proper top-flight game must be two. Yes, two paying customers attended the match between Universitatea Craiova and UM Timisoara in the Romanian First Division on 27 April 2002. (There were also 27 other onlookers and 50 policemen at the ground.) Like the stay-behinds at Old Trafford, the two hardy ticket buyers in Craiova were treated to a 0-0 draw.

⚽ Which footballers are best at acquiring native accents?

A video of Steve McClaren – the one-time England manager dubbed the wally with the brolly – went viral in August 2008, after his new club, Twente, were drawn against Arsenal in the Champions League. He sounded distinctly Dutch and spoke as if English was, at best, his second language, though to be fair, it's not the accent that is so odd but the rhythm and syntax of his speech. Unlike Joey Barton, who famously modified his Scouse tones with an *'Allo 'Allo* style French accent to address the press after he joined Marseille in 2012. The player himself dubbed this language 'Bartonese', a nice touch of self-irony, and it had a rather neat precedent in Chris Waddle's French-Geordie, perfected when he, too, played for Marseille between 1989 and 1992.

Still further back in the history of football's verbal fakery, England won the 1966 World Cup under a manager who was so worried by the hint of Essex in his dulcet tones that he would listen for hours to BBC radio announcers – this was at a time when they all spoke that form of upper class English known as Received Pronunciation – and modulate his tones to sound like them. Sir Alf never quite mastered this new accent. Before the World Cup, on a visit to Pinewood studios, Ramsey had his England players in stitches by saying hello to 007 star 'Seen' Connery.

'Eet ees deeffeecult ... we must try ter be burld." Joey Barton reinvents Franglais at Marseille.

Foreign footballers have a rather better record in adapting to regional British accents – and Danish footballers are the acknowledged masters of the genre. Peter Schmeichel grew distinctly Mancunian during his time at United, while Jan Mølby's perfected his Scouse, the midfield visionary insisted, through all the years he changed next to Sammy Lee in the dressing room. Peter Lovenkrands developed such a striking Glaswegian accent in his six years at Rangers that it has its own appreciation society on Facebook. Didi Hamann's Scouse-German accent is also unforgettable, if not quite on a par with the Danes' efforts. And nobody who heard him intervieweed could forget Jeremy Aliadiere, whose accent at Middlesbrough could go from Cockney sparrow to thoughtful Frenchman in three syllables.

🌐 What was the top pop hit by a footballer?

Let's make it immediately clear: this isn't an excuse to celebrate former Brentford centre-half Rod Stewart who played football on the *Top Of The Pops* stage with his band The Faces when 'Maggie May' was a UK number one in October 1971 and has since collaborated on two Scotland World Cup hits.

Though it lingers disturbingly long in our collective pop cultural memory, Hoddle and Waddle's 'Diamond Lights', written by Bob Puzey, only reached number 12 in 1987. Puzey's biggest hit was the Nolans' 'I'm In The Mood For Dancing' but Waddle wasn't in the mood for anything, the master of the stepover looking petrified on the nation's screens. Of the parties involved – Waddle, Hoddle, the producers, the presenters, the dancers in the studio and us, the record-buying public – the only one who didn't seem embarrassed by the whole business was Hoddle. They did at least do better than permed pop-football sensation Kevin Keegan whose 'Heads Over Heels In Love' had stalled at number 31 in 1979 in the UK, though it made the top ten in Germany.

This was no surprise. The Germans had all but invented the spine-chilling genre of singing footballers. In 1965, 1860 Munich's Yugoslav goalkeeper Petar 'Radi' Radenković, reached No 5 in the German charts, selling 400,000 copies of 'Bin i Radi, bin i König' ('Am I Radi, Am I King'). It's as atrocious as you would expect but Radenković did know something about music. His father had made his name as a folk singer under the stage name of Rascha Rodell. He was touring the US when World War Two started and never

Singing goalkeeper Petar 'Radi' Radenkovic sets the bar high for all football pop acts to follow, crooning in full strip with a Bavarian oom-pah band.

returned to Yugoslavia. Petar's brother Milan stayed in America and was known as Milan the Leather Boy after his 1967 garage rock hit 'I'm A Leather Boy'.

Making a record has been a temptation that Franz Beckenbauer, John Charles (who covered 'Sixteen Tons'), Ruud Gullit, Gerd Müller and Johan Cruyff (who, after a few, morale-boosting drinks, rose to the challenge of singing 'Oei! Oei! Oei! Dat Was Me Weer Een Loei') have all felt unable to resist. Gullit's reggae music both solo and with a band called Revelation Time is almost credible. Which is more than can be said for the biggest hit by a footballer – Paul Gascoigne's assassination of 'Fog On The Tyne (Revisited)', a UK number 2 in 1990.

⚽ Why were seven dead cats buried in a stadium in Buenos Aires?

To put a curse on a club. And it worked a treat.

The saga of what Argentinians call *Los Gatos de Racing* (the Racing Cats) begins in November 1967, when Racing Club de Avellaneda won the Intercontinental Cup in a one-game playoff against Celtic in Montevideo. Investigating the case for *When Saturday Comes* in 2002, Ben Backwell wrote: 'When Racing fans were out celebrating their World Club Championship win against Celtic, Independiente supporters entered the Racing stadium and buried seven black cats around the premises. This, for many Racing fans, is the primary reason for their disastrous performance over the following years.'

Racing Club, who had 15 league titles to their name in 1967, when the cats were buried, didn't win anything – not a trophy of any kind – for the next 35 years, while fierce local rivals Independiente ... well, let's just say they won the Copa Libertadores four times running in the 1970s, the first and still the only club to pull off this feat.

Of course the story about the cats and the curse got out, prompting Racing to start a search for the feline bodies. 'Eventually, six of the cats were found and exhumed, but the seventh could not be located,' Backwell wrote. Even an exorcism carried out by a priest and attended by 10,000 fans couldn't lift the curse – in 1998, things were so bad that the club filed for bankruptcy.

In 2001, Reinaldo Merlo (a River Plate legend who made more than 500 league appearances for the club as a defensive midfielder) became Racing's new coach. According to Backwell, he 'ordered a comprehensive search of the stadium, which

The last Racing team before the curse of the cats, photographed before the brutal 'Battle of Montevideo' (see p.53).

included digging up a moat that had been concreted over'. And that's where they finally found the remains of the seventh cat. Having lifted the curse, Racing won their 16th league title – and their first since 1966 – that very season. Merlo was nicknamed *paso a paso* ('step by step') for his insistence that the club take each game as it comes. Despite the best efforts of Merlo and other club legends such as Alfio Basile, Racing have not, however, had to expand their trophy cabinet since.

As outlandish as all this sounds, it is not that rare in football. In March 2005, Sunderland blamed a ghost after their eight game winning streak was ended by defeat to Reading. They were happily chasing promotion to the Premier League until a spectre – described by one witness as 'a strange black shape' – was glimpsed at the training ground, next to a stream called Cut Throat Dene. One player ran off in terror and striker Marcus Stewart insisted: 'Stephen Elliott is adamant he's seen something.' Although two physios pursued the figure, the mystery was never solved. At least the players weren't spooked for long: they recovered in time to clinch the Championship.

If the crisis had persisted, Sunderland might have been well-advised to call in Aguib Sosso, a West African guru of juju who allegedly helped France win the 1998 World Cup. Malian witch doctor Adama Kone insisted that Sosso 'made wrist bands for the players to ward off the evil spirits'. Indeed, if you look at photos of the French squad celebrating their triumph, you can see the wrist bands.

As it turned out, Sosso's intervention may well have been unnecessary. Before the Seleção had set off for France, centre-back Júnior Baiano had consulted his aunt, a voodoo priestess, who warned him: 'Things may not go well in the squad.' And so it proved, with Ronaldo having a mysterious breakdown on the day of the final. Apparently, he hadn't felt his usual self since he'd failed to clear his bowels before the opening game against Scotland – a ritual, designed to expel fears, initiated by Roberto Rivelino when Brazil won the 1970 World Cup. Here again, Sosso (who died in 2002) tried to take the credit, telling Kone: 'I chanted Ronaldo's name over and over again – and the spell was cast.'

⚽ How common is it for footballers to smoke?

In the mid-1980s, Juventus's iconic owner Gianni Agnelli paid one of his regular visits to the dressing room and was shocked to find Michel Platini sitting on the bench in front of his locker puffing away on a cigarette. Recognising Agnelli's consternation, Platini told him: 'You shouldn't be worried if I smoke as long as Bonini doesn't – because he is also doing the running for me.' (If anything, Platini was doing Massimo Bonini a disservice: the midfielder also did most of the running for Zbigniew Boniek.)

Platini was hardly the only great player to enjoy a smoke. Johan Cruyff's nicotine habit was so ingrained that, as a player for Ajax and Barcelona, he typically had a cigarette in the dressing room before a match, a second at half-time, a third when he returned to the dressing room after the final whistle and a fourth when he emerged from the shower. Hennes Weisweiler, the German coach who had nurtured the swashbuckling Borussia Mönchengladbach side of the 1970s, challenged him over his habit when he was managing Barcelona in 1975 and quickly found himself out of a job. Even as coach, Cruyff smoked around 20 cigarettes a day until his doctors finally made him see reason. Remarking that 'Football has given me everything in life, tobacco almost took it all away,' the Dutchman gave up Camel cigarettes for lollipops.

The commercial synergy between smoking and football stretches back to 1896 when Manchester firm Marcus & Company published the first cigarette cards with footballers on them. This seemed a natural development, as smoking was prevalent in the game at that time. In John Powles's book *Iron In The Blood*, about the origins of West Ham United, he quotes a journalist's dismayed report after one London League match in the late nineteenth century: 'I am not an anti-tobacconist but I do not think it is at all good form for a goalkeeper to be seen smoking a cigarette in goal while a game is in progress, and for a linesman to be seen smoking a pipe.'

After World War I, Manchester United legend Charlie Roberts launched a wholesale tobacconist company and

STANLEY MATTHEWS, Blackpool's quicksilver outside-right, has been capped for England no less than 33 times. Stan takes his training very seriously and soon discovered the cigarette which suited him best. "It wasn't till I changed to Craven 'A'," he says, "that I learnt what smooth smoking meant."

"The cigarette for me"

SAYS FOOTBALL GENIUS **STANLEY MATTHEWS**

EVERY WEEK crowds warm to the brilliant technical play of master-schemer Stan Matthews—football's greatest name to fans and players alike. Like so many leading sportsmen Stan's a Craven 'A' smoker. "For a really satisfying cigarette that's kind to your throat," he says, "give me a Craven 'A' every time."

P.S. *That cork tip really does make a difference, you know. There's a lot more pleasure in a cigarette with an end that's always clean, and dry, and firm between your lips*

CRAVEN 'A' smooth, <u>clean</u> smoking

Sir Stanley, despite the claims of Craven A, wasn't actually a smoker.

invented a cigarette that he called 'Ducrobel' to honour himself and two former team-mates, Dick Duckworth and Alec Bell. In the 1930s, Everton legend Dixie Deans promoted budget Carreras Clubs while in the 1950s, Stanley Matthews advertised Craven A. In one famous advert, a smiling Matthews holds a cigarette above a caption that notes: 'Stan takes his training very seriously and soon discovered the cigarette which suited him best. "It wasn't till I changed to Craven A," he says, "that I learnt what smooth smoking means."' Luckily for Blackpool, England and Stoke City, Matthews was ahead of his time in his attention to diet and lifestyle and didn't smoke.

Attitudes to tobacco in the English game had already begun to change in the 1920s and 1930s as managers such as

Frank Buckley and Herbert Chapman made their disapproval clear. Yet even as powerful a manager as Chapman had to compromise. In 1928, he smashed the British transfer record to pay £10,890 to buy forward David Jack. It was, Chapman said later, 'one of the best bargains' he ever made. Jack won three league titles with the Gunners and scored 124 goals for them. Not bad given that he smoked 25 a day.

England's World Cup winning brothers, Bobby and Jack Charlton, were smokers. There's a lovely photograph of Jack Charlton on the Leeds United training ground, dragging on a cigarette as if his life depended on it. Jack's indulgence is less surprising than Bobby's. The clean-cut United idol, revered by a generation of English schoolboys, smoked ten cigarettes a day in the 1960s but, as *Woman* magazine noted, 'never before 2pm when training was finished.' Gradually, in England, the message that tobacco is bad for a player's lungs, heart and performance, seemed to sink home. However, when Fabien Barthez joined Manchester United that same year, Sir Alex Ferguson said: 'I know Fabien smokes. He is the third United player to have been hooked on cigarettes since I've been at the club. Before him, there were Jesper Olsen and goalkeeper Les Sealey. In England, it's a rare thing to see a player smoking but, all in all, I prefer that to an alcoholic.'

That seems to be the attitude in the rest of Europe. In Italy, Platini's habit was hardly exceptional. The likes of Carlo Ancelotti, Mario Balotelli, Marcello Lippi and Gianluca Vialli all indulged. When Balotelli was at Manchester City, his manager Roberto Mancini urged the player to kick his habit of five or six ciggies a day. Such consumption would hardly impress such 40-a-day-men as European Cup-winning, Croatian midfielder Robert Prosinecki, or nonchalant genius Socrates who captained the greatest

Brazilian side never to win the World Cup (in 1982) and was also a qualified doctor.

The greatest chain-smoker in the history of the game may well be Gérson, the midfield general in Brazil's beautiful World Cup winning side of 1970. Before the tournament, the coaching staff had begged him to cut down his 60-a-day habit. He tried but admitted later that he'd failed so badly the coaches realised he was a lost cause. Gérson's failure would have been painfully obvious to anyone near the players' tunnels when Brazil were playing because, at the end of each half, he ran off the pitch and gratefully accepted a lit cigarette from one of the coaching staff. None of this prevented him from scoring Brazil's second goal in the final – restoring their lead after Italy equalised – or being so effective in that tournament as a playmaker that some fans argue he was a bigger influence in that team than Pelé.

⚽ What's behind those Stadiums of Light?

Actually, Benfica's famous Estádio da Luz goes by many names. When it was opened, in late 1954, it was known as Estádio de Carnide (after the neighbourhood of Lisbon in which the ground is sited) and was officially called Estádio do Sport Lisboa e Benfica (after the full name of the club), while many fans simply referred to it as 'The Cathedral'.

Just a brisk walk from the stadium, maybe 600 yards north, is a church called Igreja de Nossa Senhora da Luz, which translates as 'Church of Our Lady of the Light'. Listed as a national monument, the church has lent its name to many of the surrounding streets and alleys and to the parish, which is simply called Luz. Soon people began to refer to the ground as Estádio da Luz, which you could indeed translate into English as Stadium of Light, though what gets lost in the process is the precise meaning of 'light' in this context, namely God's eternal presence. (As in Hank Williams' famous gospel song 'I Saw the Light'.)

Estádio da Luz is still commonly used for the new Benfica stadium, which opened in late 2003 on the site of the old one. And the Stadium of Light is also, strangely, the name of a football ground in deeply protestant Sunderland, where the name is a reference to the lights local miners wore on their helmets. Sunderland's reborn stadium opened in 1997, on the site of the closed Monkwearmouth Colliery, and replaced the club's old Victorian ground at Roker Park.

Twenty-eight years before, on BBC television, *Monty Python's Flying Circus* had, with amusing prescience, spoofed football punditry in a sketch reflecting on the latest action in the Philosophers' Football Match at Jarrow United's Stadium of Light. The commentator/interviewer, Eric Idle quizzed John Cleese's nonplussed footballer Jimmy Buzzard after declaring, 'Last night in the Stadium of Light, Jarrow, we witnessed the resuscitation of a great footballing tradition, when Jarrow United came of age, in a European sense, with an almost Proustian display of modern existentialist football virtually annihilating by midfield moral argument the now surely obsolescent *catenaccio* defensive philosophy of Signor Alberto Fanffino.'

The one ground in the world that has most right to be called the Stadium of Light stands in Eindhoven. It's the home of what used to be the company side of the largest manufacturer of lighting on the planet but is known, in a masterful display of literal thinking, as the Philips Stadium.

Why are Italian fans called tifosi?

The term *tifosi* comes from the Italian expression *tifo sportive* which describes the social phenomenon of people developing an extreme passion for an athlete or a team. It has been suggested in Italy that the first part of the term – *tifo* – harks back to the Greek typhus (smoke, steam) but as John Foot notes in his history of Italian football, *Calcio*, it most likely comes from the medical term *tifico* (typhoid), stemming from the Greek word 'typhos'. As Foot writes: 'Sporting fans were linked to a kind of mental epidemic, which was contagious and produced forms of confusion typical of the illness ... Like football supporting, typhoid came and went in cycles.'

In a nice autobiographical piece, a blogger called Danielle, a Canadian-born freelance writer living in Italy, says: 'When I was a little girl, the word *tifosi* was almost sacred to me. In my mind it implied a higher bond with the team, more so than just a regular fan. Stereotypical *tifosi* are loud, colourful and often drink alcohol.' Then she adds: 'They are usually sporting a Ferrari shirt.' The *tifosi* she is writing about are diehard Ferrari supporters. In Italy, the word is not exclusively reserved for football fans. Birgit Schönau's book about Italian football culture (also called *Calcio*) suggests that the expression was coined by an Italian sportswriter in the 1920s to describe the feverish atmosphere at some football grounds. At that time, the potentially lethal typhoid fever, caused by the bacterium *Salmonella typhi*, was still a scourge in Italy's poorer regions. At the same time, Italian football fans in that decade were highly politicised: in 1925, there was a famous, bloody street battle between left-wing Genoa fans and fascist Bologna supporters. (Benito Mussolini didn't like football much, it wasn't manly enough, but he liked the adulation of the game's fans.)

So *tifosi* didn't originally refer to enthusiastic and exuberant fans, slightly batty in a charming way. That may be how we now associate with the term but it was coined to describe very dangerous people.

⚽ Who was the first football TV commentator?

Probably Hans-Günther Marek, one of the announcers for the Paul Nipkow Berlin TV station at the 1936 Olympics. Nipkow's live coverage of the Games, the first live coverage of an event in the history of television, ran from 10am to noon, 3pm to 7pm and 8pm to 10pm and Marek handled all the important stuff – such as Hitler's entrance and the arrival of the Olympic flame – at the Olympic stadium, where two cameras did their best to capture the action. That important stuff would have included, on 10 August 1936 at 5pm, the football semi-final between Italy and Norway. As the game went into extra time, past the 7pm cut-off, viewers may not have known the outcome: Italy won 2-1 thanks to a 96th-minute strike by Annibale Frossi.

One famous photograph of Marek shows him resplendent in a white suit, poised in front of a microphone, looking every inch the ambitious young Nazi. (In World War II he was last heard of heading up Germany's radio service in Norway.) He probably had more influence than any commentator since on the coverage of the game as, with no monitor to see what his cameramen were doing, he just described what he regarded as the most interesting action, hoping the cameras would follow his lead.

Just over a year later, on 16 September 1937, the BBC broadcast parts of a match between Arsenal and Arsenal

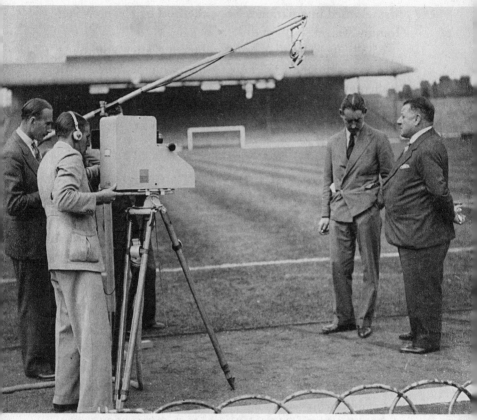

TV pundit and Arsenal manager George Allison debates the isssues of the day for the BBC with Thomas Woodroffe, 1935.

Reserves – even though there were fewer than 10,000 television sets in UK homes at that time. Arsenal manager George Allison introduced his players in that historic broadcast and he was behind the microphone on 9 April 1938 when the BBC broadcast the England v Scotland game. Allison had commentated for BBC Radio for years and was joined by a former naval officer called Thomas Woodroffe who had covered the 1936 Olympics. Scotland won the first televised international 1-0 with a goal by Hearts striker Tommy Walker.

Woodroffe is most famous for observing, after 29 minutes of extra time in the 1938 FA Cup final with the score at 0-0, 'If there's a goal scored now, I'll eat my hat.' Within seconds, George Mutch scored for Preston from the spot. Woodroffe kept his word, in a way: according to *Time* magazine, he ate a hat made of cake.

🌑 Was the soccer war about soccer?

Not really. Certainly the event that ignited the brief conflict between El Salvador and Honduras in 1969 was a World Cup qualifying tie, which is why the Polish writer and tale-teller Ryszard Kapuscinski called his account *The Soccer War* – but the underlying tensions between the neighbouring Central American countries had little to do with football.

The root causes of the war were geography and population. Honduras, with a population of 7.7m, has a territory of 43,278 square miles. El Salvador has almost as many people – 6.2m – but is less than a fifth of the size of Honduras. Inevitably, many Salvadorans spilled over a not terribly well-defined border into Honduran territory – 300,000 of them by 1969. That year, a series of two-year accords that tried to regulate this flow of people ended and was not renewed. The Honduran government also passed a new law reforming the agrarian sector which ejected some Salvadoran squatters from their land. Others fled Honduras fearing persecution. Images of their flight prompted predictably jingoistic rhetoric from Salvadoran politicians.

So when the two countries' teams met in a World Cup qualifier on 8 June 1969 in the Honduran capital, Tegucigalpa, the match had taken on titanic symbolic importance.

Honduras won the first match 1-0. A few rival supporters fought in the stands and the visitors left convinced that they had been cheated, with the winning goal scored in the tenth minute of injury time. By the time the second leg was played a week later, the outrage in El Salvador had become so intense that the police had to hide the Honduran team in a secret location outside the capital, San Salvador. Three Salvadorans died in riots before the match. With the police confiscating booze and weapons on the way into the stadium, the match was almost an anti-climax. Salvador won 3-0. This meant that both teams were level on points and, with neither goal difference or aggregate scores being used as tie-breaker, the two sides would meet again in a play-off.

This was the last thing either country needed. Rocks were thrown at some Honduran fans' cars as they drove back home. The Honduran government exaggerated these incidents, even suggesting that the Salvadorans were holding Hondurans prisoner. Such stories provoked attacks on Salvadoran communities. Soon, as many as 1,400 refugees a day were crossing the border, seeking sanctuary in El Salvador.

With troops skirmishing on the border, the Salvadoran Council of Ministers accused the Honduran government of 'the crime of genocide'. Diplomatic relations were broken off a few days after the play-off, in Mexico City on 26 June, which El Salvador won 3-2.

The football was over but the war was about to begin. On 3 July, a small Honduran plane flew over Salvadoran territory. Eleven days later, three Honduran fighters flew into Salvadoran air space in the morning. By that afternoon, Salvador had struck back, bombing Tegucigalpa airport and sending troops across the border.

The war lasted about 100 hours, long enough to kill somewhere between 2,000 and 6,000 people. Peace didn't officially break out until the warring neighbours signed a treaty in 1980. By then El Salvador was engulfed by a far deadlier conflict: a civil war between the right-wing government and its opposition in which 75,000 Salvadorans died.

Reaching the 1970 World Cup finals was a milestone for El Salvador. But they finished bottom of Group A, having scored no goals and losing all three games. The highlight, if you can call it that, of the campaign came in the second match against hosts Mexico. The Salvadorans had held their own, with midfielder Mauricio Rodríguez hitting the post. Then, just before half-time, they were awarded a free-kick by Egyptian referee Hussaian Kandil. For no obvious reason, Mexican defender Mario Peréz decided to take it, passing the ball to Aarón Padilla who crossed for Javier Valdivia to make it 1-0. As Brian Glanville noted: 'In vain did the El Salvador players argue, weep and lie on the ground. The goal disgracefully stood. Mexico went on to score three more against a demoralised side.'

Twelve years later, Luis Ramírez Zapata scored El Salvador's first goal in a World Cup finals. His celebrations were slightly muted by the fact that his side were already losing 5-0 when he scored and would go on to lose 10-1, a record defeat in a World Cup finals. Such is the misery this Central American nation has endured in World Cups, it is a wonder they still enter.

Acknowledgements

Thanks to Alison Ratcliffe, Andrew Murphy, Martin Mazur. Paolo Menicucci, Jack Simpson, Lesley Simpson, Philippe Auclair, Simon Kanter, Helen Morgan, Jonathan Wilson, Susanne Hillen and Henry Iles.

Photo credits

While every effort has been made to contact copyright-holders of illustrations, the author and publishers would be grateful for information about any illustrations where they have been unable to trace them, and would be glad to make amendments in further editions.

The following images are copyright Getty Images: pages iv, 4, 13, 16, 18, 22, 29, 33, 35, 41, 49, 53, 57, 70, 87, 89, 95, 97, 103, 111, 114, 116, 119, 121, 126, 130, 137, 141, 145, 147, 150, 153, 155, 157, 159, 165, 169, 173, 175, 181, 187, 190, 197, 200, 203, 209, 213, 224, 29, 243, 251, 271.

Index

About the authors

PAUL SIMPSON was launch editor of *FourFourTwo* magazine. He is the author of the critically acclaimed *Rough Guide to Elvis* and currently edits the UEFA magazine, *Champions*. His favourite football team of all time is Jimmy Bloomfield's Leicester City.

ULI HESSE is the author of *Tor! The Story of German Football*, a contributor to 11 Freunde magazine and is writing a book on the history of Borussia Dortmund, the club he supports, through the eyes of its fans. He has written more than 300 columns for ESPN FC.